The Metaphor of Play

The Metaphor of Play

Disruption and Restoration in the Borderline Experience

by

Russell Meares

Jason Aronson Inc.
Northvale, New Jersey
London

The author gratefully acknowledges permission to reprint material from the following sources:

"The Fragile Spielraum," by Russell Meares, copyright © 1990 by the Analytic Press, and "Reversals: On Certain Pathologies of Identification," copyright © 1993 by the Analytic Press. Both chapters appear in *Progress in Self Psychology*, edited by A. Goldberg. Reprinted by permission of A. Goldberg and the publisher.

"Transference and the Playspace," by Russell Meares, in *Contemporary Psychoanalysis*, vol. 28, no. 1, edited by A. Feiner. Copyright © 1992 by the William Alanson White Institute. Reprinted by permission.

"On Self-Boundary: A Study of the Development of the Concept of Secrecy," by Russell Meares and Wendy Orlay, in *British Journal of Medical Psychology*, vol. 61, pp. 305–316. Copyright © 1988 by The British Psychological Society.

Excerpts from *The Nature of Mind*, by David Armstrong. Copyright © 1981 by David Armstrong. Reprinted by permission of David Armstrong.

Production Editor: Judith D. Cohen

This book was set in 11-point Palacio by Lind Graphics of Upper Saddle River, New Jersey, and printed and bound by Haddon Craftsmen of Scranton, Pennsylvania.

Copyright © 1993 by Jason Aronson Inc.

10 9 8 7 6 5 4 3 2 1

Library of Congress Cataloging-in-Publication Data

Meares, Russell.
   The metaphor of play : disruption and restoration in the borderline experience / by Russell Meares.
       p.   cm.
   Includes bibliographical references and index.
   ISBN 0-87668-275-1 (hard cover)
   1. Borderline personality disorder.   2. Selflessness (psychology)—
Treatment.   3. Play—Therapeutic use.   I. Title.
   [DNLM: 1. Borderline Personality Disorder—therapy.   2. Play and
Playthings.   3. Self Concept.   WM 190 M483m]
   RC569.5.B67M43 1993
   616.85'852—dc20
   DNLM/DLC
   for Library of Congress   92-49186

Manufactured in the United States of America. Jason Aronson Inc. offers books and cassettes. For information and catalog write to Jason Aronson Inc., 230 Livingston Street, Northvale, New Jersey 07647.

CONTENTS

ACKNOWLEDGMENTS

I was very fortunate that when I first came to think about the subject of this book, it was in the company of Robert Hobson. Our conversations and friendship, which began in London on his unit specializing in what is now called the "borderline" personality, have continued for the last twenty-seven years. They have provided an essential background and "scaffolding" for the development of the main thesis of this book.

A second major influence was my father, Ainslie Meares. He was a pioneer of the view that in most patients, significant change does not come about through "insight." Writing in *The Lancet* (1961, 1962) of his experiences working with seriously ill people, he concluded that recovery seemed to be related to the physician's understanding of his patient. He considered that the main healing effect comes through the therapist's fostering a form of mental activity that is nonlinear, nonlogical, and that is found in states such as reverie. This state is broken into by moments of anxiety, so that the principal therapeutic task is to deal with these intrusions of anxiety in order to allow the healing form of mental function to begin again. This approach conforms, in broad outline, to that based on the metaphor of the play space.

I was thirdly fortunate in meeting Bernard Brandchaft. I am grateful to him for his generosity, for the pleasure of our discussions, and for the stimulus they provided.

Fourth, I thank my colleagues at Westmead Hospital for their support during the writing of this book. Dr. Robert Gordon, in particular, was a constant source of invaluable encouragement. We have developed at Westmead a program for the psychotherapy of severe personality disorder. In essence, this book described the model upon which the treatment is based. The program includes an evaluative component. The initial outcome data have recently been reported (Stevenson and Meares 1992). I have greatly appreciated my partnership with Dr. Janine Stevenson in this venture. Many people in Sydney, Melbourne, Perth, Hobart, and also New Zealand, whom I have supervised over the last ten years, have provided germs of ideas that eventually found their way into the text. I thank them all. I am especially grateful to Dr. Josephine Anderson, Ms. Trish Coombes, Dr. Jill Floyd, Ms. Trudy McKay, Dr. Antony Milch, Ms. Tessa Phillips, Dr. Neil Schultz, Dr. Marie Shaw, Dr. Andrew Singer, Dr. Sue Thompson, and Dr. Peter Wigg. Karina Bray has been helpful in giving advice about developmental studies.

I am grateful to Dr. A. Feiner and Dr. A. Goldberg, editors, respectively, of *Contemporary Psychoanalysis* and *Progress in Self Psychology*, for permission to reproduce material that has appeared in their publications. The papers concerned are: "Transference and the Play Space: Towards a New Basic Metaphor," *Contemporary Psychoanalysis*, 1992, 28:32–49; and "The Fragile Spielraum," *Progress in Self Psychology*, Vol. 6, 1990, and "Reversals: On Certain Pathologies of Identification," *Progress in Self Psychology*, Vol. 9, 1993, Hillsdale, NJ: Analytic Press.

My secretary, Ms. Rhonda Joel, has displayed great patience, tenacity, and good humor in bringing the manuscript to fruition. She has provided enormous support. Finally, I thank my wife, Susanne, who in very many ways has contributed to the book. Not the least of them was the provision of the creative environment in which it could grow.

PLAY AND THE
SENSE OF SELF

Chapter 1

Those who suffer a pervasive feeling of emptiness, who live as if on the surface, caught up in a ceaseless traffic with the stimuli of the everyday world, are the main focus of this book. These people sense no core existence and are often without access to true emotions or an authentic feeling of being alive. Such disturbances of the experience of self are common. Indeed, people afflicted with them make up the bulk of those who confront a psychotherapist in the modern age. Their severity ranges from a subtle and unobtrusive disturbance of personality, to a severely disabling condition associated with repeated hospitalizations, suicide attempts, and broken relationships.

Until the 1970s, no major psychology could adequately explain the diminishment and fragility of the sense of existence that affect these people. In recent years, however, an understanding has begun to develop and is attracting increasing interest. For the first time, the most severe manifestation of the disturbance has officially been given a name—the borderline personality. The aim of this book is to show how borderline experiences can be understood and how a way of treating them can be derived from this understanding. The main theme depends upon two paradoxes. The first is that self, which is private, grows in the public domain. The second is that inner life, which we sense as insubstantial, is founded on physical things, such as toys and parts of bodies.

Ideas about self and its origins were being developed in the United States about a century ago. James Mark Baldwin was one of the proponents of ideas about self. He belonged to a group of psychologists who sought to understand self and its evolution. William James was the leading figure in this school. Like his brother Henry, the novelist, William was intrigued by the phenomena of individual consciousness and by the problem of expressing, in simple language, their intricate nature. Others in this group included Josiah Royce, Charles Cooley, and George Herbert Mead in the United States; Pierre Janet in Paris; and Edouard Claparède and others in Switzerland. They influenced each other and also gained from philosophers such as Henri Bergson.

Just before World War I, the American expression of this line of thinking was swept away in what has been called by Susan Harter (1983) a "radical behaviorist purge" (p. 226). A new era arose, in which conceptions of man and mind were peculiarly mechanical. Such notions as self that could not be touched or measured were banished from the curricula of academic psychology as unscientific, leaving a vacancy at the heart of that discipline. The dominant psychodynamic theory of the time, ego psychology, formulated a notion of mind that was consistent with the images of the late industrial age. Ego was the "psychic apparatus." This system of thinking included no notions of self until the late 1930s.[1]

These ideas seemed to be manifestations of something deeper, of a fundamental shift in the way in which those in the West conceived of themselves and of their relationship with others. This shift was reflected not only in psychology but in the physical sciences, in political thinking, and in the dominant works of artistic expression. Casimir Malevic, for example, just before World War I, began to paint images that showed the fusion of man and machine. He was followed by a series of major painters, including Umberto Boccioni in Italy, and Fernand Leger and Francis Picabia[2] in France, who portrayed man as a mechanism.

Furthermore, the dominance of linear and geometrical forms of painting over more random, wandering, and, in this way, more human forms of expression extended from Malevic through Mondrian to the Bauhaus School and on to the 1960s in New York with Barnett Newman and Kenneth Noland.

The ideas of James, Baldwin, and their colleagues could not exist in such an intellectual atmosphere, which, for heuristic purposes but not entirely fancifully, we might date from 1913 to 1971. James died in 1910. His influence waned soon after. Baldwin was forgotten. In Paris, Bergson's great books had all been written, and Janet, who before the war had seemed likely to become the greatest psychiatrist of his time, was destined to become instead a footnote in the history of psychodynamic thought, his major works never translated. Only in Switzerland did the tradition live on. In very different ways, Ludwig Binswanger and Carl Gustav Jung pursued the problems of existence and self; the developmental psychology of Jean Piaget flourished.[3] In the United States, the rout was so complete, in the field of psychology at least, that when in 1972 Arnold Buss came to study the subject of private consciousness, perhaps the most fundamental fact of which we are aware, he found no single reference to it in the literature of psychology.

The tradition began to revive in America in the 1940s under the influence of Harry Stack Sullivan, who acknowledged his debt to George Herbert Mead. It was not until the 1970s, however, that the extraordinary situation discovered by Arnold Buss began to be rectified.

The concept of *self* was welcomed back to the scientific fold. At the same time, mother–infant interaction emerged as a major field of study. It seemed that an awareness had arisen that, in some way, "self" evolved through the child's engagement with the nurturing environment. The work of Heinz Kohut in applying a psychology of self in the clinical field excited widespread interest and gained a general recognition. Kohut had arrived at his conclusions by a very different pathway from his predecessors, gaining his insights from clinical material. His explorations were paralleled in England by D. W. Winnicott, whose developmental approach was based on observations of children. This book belongs to and is indebted to this broad tradition.

The second paradox upon which the book is based, that of self as substance, first presented itself to me in a much more personal way.

About twenty-five years ago, I encountered a young woman, Miss A., a waitress, ill-educated, and intensely shy.[4] What she said was often puzzling and hard to grasp. Yet it was important, since she struggled to portray the reality in which she lived. One day she said something that seemed to be of fundamental significance. She was finding, as she usually did, that it was very difficult to talk. She tried to explain: "I suppose I'm scared that if I talk, there'll be nothing left to say. Say I told you all my thoughts, ideas, and whatsit, it'd be like me piled up beside us, with nothing left to say."

Miss A. seemed to feel that she was composed of a series of ideas and that should they be lost, she would cease to exist. It was as if she attributed concrete substance to her ideas and experienced her thoughts as the stuff of her existence. Their loss implied the threat of dematerialization. As a consequence, at our first meeting, standing in a corner of the room, she told me that she did not want to speak. Subsequently, in groups she remained silent. For her, there would be no idle chatter, since conversation served only to reveal her inner world of "thoughts, ideas, and whatsit."

Miss A. was aware that her sense of personal fragility had something to do with her relationships with others. She strove, in halting phrases, to describe this apprehension: "If I began to speak—it's too big—like stepping on a merry-go-round—no, it's like stepping stones across the sea—having to go on to the end. The stepping stones are like situations, incidents more likely. I can't quite manage them. I scramble from one to the other. How I got from this morning to here was most unpleasant. I felt things were demanded." Her inner world of thoughts and emotions was constantly demanded in the encounters of daily life, when a part of herself was shown to another person and momentarily occupied a precarious existence outside her. She implied that to expose one's thoughts is to risk a kind of personal damage, through a faulty response of others. On another occasion she seemed to say that the sense of damage was like a wound to her physical being.

The frailty of Miss A. is not shared by everyone. Nevertheless, it does seem that, for most of us, there are threads of thoughts and images that are felt as intensely personal. They are valued and perceived as a kind of inner core. They have a creative potential and are also the locus of a sense of self.

From where do such experiences come? At the heart of this book lies the idea that the play of the preschool child, and a mental activity similar to it in the adult, is necessary to the growth of a healthy self. Seen in this way, the play of the child is not mere diversion. It is vital to the evolution of mature psychic life.[5]

Play takes place in a space that is created by the atmosphere of another. The play space, part real, part illusory, provides the basic metaphor through which the experiences of Miss A. and others who suffer disorders of self might be understood.

The play of the very young child has peculiar characteristics that include the nature of the relationship with the other, the form of language, and an absorption in the activity that is similar to that of an adult who is lost in thought. The field of play is where, to a large extent, a sense of self is generated. These and related developmental ideas make up the first part of this book. The second part identifies common disruptions of this normal development. They arise through the fragility of the play space, which is easily broken up by alerting stimuli and the faulty responses of others. For a child who habitually lives in such a situation, the field of play is never adequately established, so that there is little chance to elaborate those experiences that form the core of self. The individual is left with a sense of nothing much inside, or no "real me." The final chapters describe the therapeutic approach. The task of the therapist who works within this system is, first of all, to establish, in a metaphoric sense, the field of play.

Part I | **DEVELOPMENT**

Chapter 2 | **THE SECRET**

As soon as we try to understand how a disturbance in the sense of self might come about, we strike an obstacle. What is self? How can it be defined? These difficult questions must be given some kind of answer before we go on.

An approach to the problem of conceiving so elusive and abstract an entity as self can be made in a negative way. Although it is hard to say what self is, we can say, without doubt, that it is distinct from not-self. This simple dichotomy provides a starting point. In making a distinction between self and not-self, we draw a line between not only our bodies but also a whole range of experiences, such as thoughts, feelings, and memories that are felt as one's own and as part of an inner world that is distinguished from an outer world. We are led to a fundamental idea—self depends upon the concept of *innerness*. The development of this concept is shown through the child's understanding of secrecy.

We are not born with a self. For some time, the child seems to conceive the boundary between his or her world of feelings and thoughts and the world of others as incomplete. Children seem to believe that those who are close to them will know of these feelings and thoughts, even their dreams. For example, one of Piaget's (1929) 5-year-old subjects is asked: "Could I see your dream?" "No, you would be too far away." "And your mother?" "Yes, but she lights the light" (p. 94).

Piaget (1929) wrote that "it is indispensable to establish clearly and before all else the boundary the child draws between the self and the external world" (p. 34).

Despite the evident importance of the development of self-boundary, there has been little actual study of it. We do not know, for example, the age at which the concept is attained. Mahler and colleagues (1975) suggest that it is between 2 and 3 years of age; Piaget's findings imply that it is considerably later, from 7 to 9. One supposes that the lack of data arises through difficulties inherent in studying so subtle a notion as self-boundary. Pierre Janet, however, gave us a way of approaching the problem.

Janet was the star of a school of psychiatry that was evolving in Paris toward the end of the nineteenth century. The story of his rivalry with Freud, his eclipse, and his death, which passed without public notice, is wonderfully told by Henri Ellenberger (1970). Janet's hypotheses and clinical insights, many of them brilliant, have been lost, Ellenberger points out, or are largely neglected following his fall from influence. Among his ideas was the notion that the child's discovery of the concept of secrecy is an event of enormous significance since it heralds the birth of an inner world. When the child learns that thoughts and ideas can be kept within himself and are not accessible to others, he realizes that there is some kind of demarcation between his world, which is inner, and that which is outer. Seen in this way, a study of the age at which children know what it means to keep a secret may allow us to infer the age of self-boundary formation.

We used Janet's idea in a study of forty preschool children in Western Sydney, Australia. The children came from all socio-economic groups (Meares and Orlay 1988).

The study depended upon the child's responses to a large colored photograph of two adolescents, called Cathy and Paul. Cathy was shown with her hand cupped to Paul's ear, as if she were whispering. The child was asked: "What are Cathy and Paul doing?" The questions that followed were designed to elicit the child's knowledge of and use of the word *secret*, the content of secrets, those who were recipients of secrets, and those with whom one cannot share a secret.

Another test consisted of the simple presentation of a moral dilemma in order to investigate the strategy of lying, which also seems to represent an understanding that a thought or idea can be kept hidden. The first question to each girl in the study was: "If Cathy was naughty, and her mummy asked, 'Cathy, have you been naughty?' what would Cathy say?" The same question was asked of the boys, except that it involved Paul.

The taped interviews showed fairly clearly that most children older than 4 years of age understood the notion of secrecy. Of the fourteen children younger than 4 years, only two had attained this concept. Of these two, one aged 3.5 years was regarded as exceptionally advanced; the other was aged 3.11 years. Seven of twelve children between 4.0 and 4.5 years and nine of fourteen children between 4.7 and 5.9 years understood the concept of secrecy. The range of ages for attainment of the concept was from 3.5 to 5.5 years.

The findings concerning lying were complementary and surprisingly unequivocal. On no occasion did the interviewer introduce the strategy of lying as a possible response to the dilemma. Twenty-four children, however, spontaneously recommended such a strategy. One typical response was: "She would say George did it." George was the child's brother. Lying, then, is normal in terms of the moral development of this age group, as Piaget (1932) had pointed out.

Of the sixteen children who did not lie, only seven told the truth. The predominant response of the others was to run and hide, as if the child believed that one cannot hide one's thoughts but can still hide oneself. Other responses of the nonliars included crying and asking to be cuddled.

Understanding the strategy of lying was clearly age related. The mean age of the children who lied was 4.6 years, and the nonliars, 3.11. The strategy of lying was also closely related to the attainment of the concept of secrecy. Of the nineteen children who did not understand secrecy, only five lied. Seventeen of the eighteen who understood secrecy also lied. (Three children could not be classified in terms of the secrecy concept.)

These findings suggest that at the beginning of the

fifth year of life, the large majority of children know that it is possible to avoid getting into trouble, disapproval, or punishment by lying. The fact, however, that some children lie earlier than this may not necessarily indicate the achievement of the inner-outer distinction. Although the behavior of some children might have been based on the knowledge that their thoughts were not accessible to others, other children may have adopted the strategy through imitation of an older sibling. Therefore, the results of the secrecy interview are the more fundamental data in charting the emergence of a private self.[1]

Some extracts from the tapes illustrate the children's ideas about secrets and to whom they would tell them.

Boy (4.0 years):
What are Cathy and Paul doing?
Telling secrets.
What are secrets?
You tell someone and they're not allowed to tell anyone.
Very good. What kind of things are secrets about?
Presents. Like we got a Lilo* and it wasn't even anyone's birthday.
Can secrets be about anything else?
You can pretend things, like dressing up.
Is that a secret?
Yes, because I'm a boy and I'm wearing a dress.
If that's a secret, who can you tell?
Jade, if you don't let her take the scarf, because she always wants them ALL!
Who can't you tell?
Daddy and Mummy because of the paint on my face, even if I wash it off they will be angry.
Who else can you tell?
Um, anyone but not if you don't like them, because they don't like me.
Can I tell Miss Sweeney?
Yes, she's the teacher, like you. I'll tell her, then Helen!
Girl (4.7 years)
What are Cathy and Paul doing?
Telling secrets.
What are secrets?

---

*A Lilo is an inflatable mattress used for lying on the beach or in water.

(Silence)
What is she saying to him?
(Silence)
Do you know any secrets, then?
Yes, I didn't invite Patricia to my party.
Can I tell anyone?
Anyone except Patricia. I know another secret; Boy George is a poofter. **
Why is that a secret?
Because it's a square (swear) word.
What, *poofter*?
Yes, a policeman will come and lock you up if you say it again.
Who else can't you tell secrets to?
Anyone who isn't your friend.
What about mummy and daddy?
I can tell them.
What about Miss Smythe?
No, she's the teacher.
Isn't she your friend?
No.
Why did you tell me?
Because you wear beautiful earrings, and so do I. Can you take yours off?

An example of a child who did not understand secrecy follows:

Girl (3.9 years)
What are Cathy and Paul doing?
Whispering.
Why whispering instead of talking out loud?
Because they're in a picture.
Why do people whisper?
To sound like the grass rustling.
Do you know what a secret is?
No.
Do you ever know something that no one else knows about?
No.

These extracts show that what is held secret often concerns such intensely personal matters as gender identity and ideas

---

**Poofter is a slang term for homosexual.

about forbidden sexuality. Other responses described secrets that would bring shame to the individual should they be revealed. Examples included illegitimate pregnancy and being unable to swim. Such secrets might have been predicted. What was surprising, at least to the adult mind, was that the majority of secrets involved pleasant events and valued objects, such as birthday surprises and gifts. Some of these children had learned that such secrets could be used to exchange in the formation of alliances and friendships. A treehouse was an example of such a secret. It was a treat to be offered only to friends. Secrets were given only to those to whom the child felt very close.

These children came upon a paradox. At the same time as they found that their personal worlds were distinct and separate from others, they also found a means of connectedness to others. The discovery of the notion of the secret brings about an immense change and an enlargement in the child's life. The child learns that through the emergence of a sense of privacy, groups can be formed. A shared secret unites people and, at times, gives them a common identity. They might become, for example, "the tree house tribe." This is not so merely for children. The transmission of confidences helps to develop social networks among adults (Simmel 1964). Many tribal societies depend upon systems of secrecy to hold them together. Jung (1961), who observed this phenomenon, implied that it served an important developmental function. He wrote: "The secret society is an intermediary stage on the way to individuation" (p. 342).

The attainment of the concept of secrecy brings another major change in relating to others. For the first time, intimacy, of the kind that adults share, is possible. The child begins to know that secrets are disclosed in a developing dialogue with others who can be trusted to share and respect them. The secrets then become the coins of intimacy and the currency of its transactions. In contrast, a younger child's relationships with others do not involve exchange with another whose world is known to be different and not one's own. Rather, the small child lives in a single, personal universe of which the parents constitute a major part. They are close in that the child is devastated by their absence, but they are not conceived as having peculiarly individual wishes, feelings, or memories that differ from the child's. Flavell (1968) demonstrated this in a number of ways; for example, children were shown several objects (stockings, necktie, adult book, toy truck, and doll). They were asked to choose gifts for their parents, their siblings, and themselves. The 3-year-olds tended to give parents gifts they would like themselves, so that mother would be offered a toy truck. Some 4-year-olds, half the 5-year-olds, and all the children of 6 chose appropriate gifts. The attainment of self-boundary allows not only the formation of intimate relations, but also the feeling of empathy. Predictably, those who suffer severe personality disorder have deficiencies in both areas. They tend to make nonintimate attachments and have relationships in which the others feel exploited. They also suffer what might be termed *pathologies of privacy*.

Pathologies of privacy are shown in subtle ways. They are not obvious at first contact, nor is the individual usually aware of them. One category of disturbance depends upon a precarious and ill-developed sense of innerness. Since what is inner is minimal and unstable, it cannot be exposed to the risk of a faulty response or some diminishment at the hand of others. These people have grave difficulties in telling others of their deepest feelings, their profoundest wishes, and their imaginings. In order to preserve a core of personal experience, which seems necessary to the sense of self, the individual develops strategies, often unconsciously, that hide this highly valued interior zone. These strategies may be complex, for the danger of exposure has to be balanced against the need for intimacy, in which revelation is required. An extreme resolution of this dilemma may be the use of false secrets as the currency of an intimate relationship (Meares 1976).

A second kind of pathology of privacy might be called *psychic incontinence*. The individual is rather like the child who does not yet conceive of an inner world. An example was provided by a young woman who remarked that she had difficulty in expressing her feelings, except when she was using the telephone. Her therapist, however, soon found that she *was* expressive. She let him know immediately whatever she felt. He was not alone. Her workmates had learned so much of her feelings and of her intermittent despair, which sometimes led to self-mutilation, that they patrolled the restroom to make sure no harm had come to her. Her exasperated family were spared no details of her therapeutic sessions. In some ways, she was like a child who has no secrets. In contrast, it seemed that she did not like this state and in some part of her there was a wish to move beyond it. She hated it when her therapist put into words the emotion she was currently experiencing. Moreover, she disliked being looked at, as if the observer could too easily read her emotions. Her curious preference for telephone conversations now seemed less puzzling. In this way she could escape the feeling that others would inevitably know what was going on inside her.

Although we have so far considered the importance of the concept of privacy in the evolution of intimacy, the child's attainment of this milestone brings with it other major changes, one of which can be inferred from the following story.

A 5-year-old child in Victorian England discovered that his father did not know of a misdemeanor that the child had recently committed. With this discovery, a sudden realization swept over the youngster. Years later he (Gosse 1907) wrote of the immense import of this experience:

> Of all the thoughts which rushed upon my savage and undeveloped little brain at this crisis, the most curious was that I had found a companion and a confidant in myself. There was a secret in this world and it belonged to me and to somebody who lived in the same body with me. There were two of us, and we could talk with one another. It is difficult to define impressions so rudimentary, but it is certain that it was in this dual form that the sense of my individuality now suddenly descended upon me, and it is equally certain that it was a great solace to me to find a sympathizer in my own breast. [p. 58]

This incident from the autobiography of Edmund Gosse illustrates not only the importance of the development of an idea of secrecy for the achievement of a sense of individuality, but also that this individuality is dual. The dualisms that emerge with the concept of privacy are multiple. First, there is a distinction between subject and object in the social world; others are not merely parts of a personal universe. Second, there is a distinction between thoughts of things and those things themselves. Third, there is an awareness of a dualism in the inner world in which also subject and object are sensed. This idea is central to an understanding of the growth of self. It will be touched upon in later chapters.

These changes are universal and part of ordinary psychic evolution. Sometimes, however, the attainment of the concept of an inner life brings with it a development that is peculiarly individual. It arises from the fact that those ideas, feelings, images, memories, and fantasies that make up the inner world are not all given the same value. Some, which concern things that are commonly sensed, are passed about in small talk and gossip. Others are highly valued and sensed as a kind of inner core. They may form the germ or seed out of which grows an individual life. This idea is illustrated by the story of Richard St. Barbe Baker, who achieved international fame for his work on the conservation of the world's forests.

In a radio broadcast[3] made at the age of 91, St. Barbe Baker described an occasion during childhood when, for some reason, he had wandered away from home into a neighboring wood. Although he was only 4 years old and lost, he was filled with a sense of the marvelous, as if he were in a dream. He came to a clearing, where he sat for a while. Sounds were amplified so that the crack of a breaking twig was like the lash of a cartwhip and birdsong sounded like organ notes. As he listened, he heard the tinkling of a brook, which he followed, and so found his way home.

Although he went back to the same place the next day, he could not recapture the feeling of wonder and excitement. Nevertheless, the clearing in the forest now had significance. He often returned to it. He said,

> Sometimes when things had gone wrong during the day, which wasn't infrequent, I used to escape from the house and go to the beechwood and I'd put my hands on the smooth bark. It was like my mother confessor. Everything seemed to be cleaned up—all the troubles of the day vanished and I went back to the house. I generally managed to slip in without being noticed by anybody. But one occasion my father caught me going into his study by the door through the conservatory. And he said, "My dear boy where have you been?" "Oh, daddy, I've been out to see the stars. It's a wonderful night, come out." But I'd never give away my story, I'd never tell people where I went and I never gave away the secret of my mother confessor, my Madonna of the Woods.

The soothing aspect of the secret, reminiscent of the effect of the mother, is evident in this story. Its whole effect, however, extended far beyond it. This incident became the germinal center out of which grew the direction and shaping of an entire life. The discovery and creative elaboration of such a secret, as yet unrealized and perhaps only dimly conscious, becomes an ideal goal toward which a therapy is aimed.

Chapter 3 | **SELF AS DOUBLE**

Although we may say that the birth of self comes with the discovery of what a secret means, this discovery is built on a past and on earlier, embryonic forms of self. We must know something of the nature of this history to understand disorders of self. To explore this development, it is first necessary to describe self somewhat more completely. I approach this matter with the help of Australian philosopher David Armstrong.

Armstrong (1981) writes in a clear and straightforward way. He asks us to consider the experience of the long-distance truck driver. I use his own words:

> After driving for long periods of time, particularly at night, it is possible to "come to" and realize that for some time past one has been driving without being aware of what one has been doing. The coming-to is an alarming experience. It is natural to describe what went on before one came to by saying that during that time one lacked consciousness. Yet it seems clear that, in the two senses of the word that we have so far isolated, consciousness was

present. There was mental activity, and as part of that mental activity, there was perception. That is to say, there was minimal consciousness and perceptual consciousness. [p. 59]

The truck driver responded to stimuli, both meaningful and meaningless. Lest we doubt this, Armstrong goes on to describe the sophistication of the truck driver's activities while he apparently lacked awareness. He suggests that many animals may be operating by means of the two forms of consciousness assumed for the truck driver—namely, *minimal,* involving some kind of mental activity, and *perceptual,* concerning the capacity to perceive. A complex neurophysiological apparatus is at work that deals with environmental events in an appropriate way. But there is no self in it. As Armstrong (1981) puts it, "There is an important sense, we are inclined to think, in which he has no experiences, indeed is not really a person" (p. 63). The truck driver functions like many animals and also like the infant, whose perceptual and organizational abilities are evident in the first few weeks of life. For the truck driver to experience a sense of self, another kind of consciousness, which is presumably a later evolutionary development, is needed. Seen in this way, it is only likely to be found in few, if any, animals and at a relatively late stage in human development. This kind of consciousness is *introspective consciousness.*

When the truck driver "comes to," something happens that is analogous to a light going on in utter darkness. He begins to reflect upon his experience. Armstrong remarks that this

> introspective consciousness is bound up in a quite special way with consciousness of self. I do not mean that the self is one of the particular objects of introspective awareness alongside our mental states and activities. This view was somewhat tentatively put forward by [Bertrand] Russell in *Problems of Philosophy* (1912, ch. 5), but it had already been rejected by Hume and Kant. It involves accepting the extraordinary view that what seems most inward to us, our mental states and activities, are not really us. What I mean, rather, is that we take the states and activities of which we are introspectively aware to be states and activities of a single continuing thing. [p. 65]

Armstrong concludes that "introspective consciousness is consciousness of self" (p. 67).

The intricacies of Armstrong's argument will not be encompassed here. Nevertheless, a final aspect from his argument is important. It concerns memory. Armstrong argues that the truck driver while in his unconscious state functioned like an infant in terms of memory. The various stimuli along the road presumably triggered certain kinds of memories that enabled him to respond appropriately. He was stimulus-bound, living solely in the present. On his recovery of introspective consciousness, he had little recollection of what was happening while it was absent. "It is tempting to suppose, therefore, as a psychological hypothesis, that unless mental activity is monitored by introspective consciousness, then it is not remembered to have occurred, or at least it is unlikely that it will be remembered" (p. 67).

Armstrong concludes his argument in the following way:

> The two parts of the argument now may be brought together. If introspective consciousness involved (in reasonably mature human beings) consciousness of self, and if without introspective consciousness there would be little or no memory of the past history of the self, the apparent special illumination and power of introspective consciousness is explained. Without introspective consciousness, we would not be aware that we existed—our self would not be self to itself. [p. 67]

This idea is essential to my story. The notion of introspective consciousness implies a kind of spatiality of personal experience in which there is a sense of distance between consciousness itself and the contents of consciousness. There is a doubleness in this experience that, as the story from the childhood of Edmund Gosse suggests, is not to be found in infancy.

In the very beginning of life, we suppose that very many experiences are adualistic and have no self in them, in Armstrong's sense. There are probably times when the baby is, as it were, simply inhabited by sensation. An adult may imagine this adualism by using the memory of those rare occasions in which the intensity of experiences presses upon him or her as if to fill up all personal space. In extreme anxiety, for example, we are aware only of terror, a beating heart, tension in muscles, and other immediate sensations. There seems to be no distance between these experiences and our awareness of them. We cannot, as it were, stand back from them, look at them, and evaluate what is happening. In the same way, the baby is relatively stimulus bound, acting in a reflexive way, as if in the grip of immediate sensation, with no perspective upon it. For example, the young baby grasps at everything, as if instinctively. For the baby, we might say that the doubleness of personal existence is found in the engagement with the mother. This subject is approached in the following chapter.

Armstrong's argument concerning the doubleness of personal existence was anticipated by William James. In considering ordinary experience expressed in ordinary language, James found our consciousness to be "duplex." We are aware of the things of the outer world and also of the images and other elements of our inner life. There is a difference, however, between the awareness, or consciousness, and those things of which we are aware. James (1892) describes this duality in the following way:

> Whatever I may be thinking of, I am always at the same time more or less aware of *myself*, of my *personal existence*. At the same time, it is I who am aware; so that the total self of me, being as it were duplex, partly known and partly knower, partly object and partly subject, must have two aspects discriminated in it, of which for shortness we may call one the *Me* and the other the *I*. I call these "discriminated aspects," and not separate things, because the identity of *I* with *me*, even in the very act of their discrimination, is perhaps the most ineradicable dictum of commonsense and must not be undermined by our terminology here at the outset, whatever we may come to think of its validity at our inquiry's end. [p. 176]

The distinction by James between the *I* and the *Me* and the perspective of one upon the other is a fundamental one and central to the main thesis of this book. In the simplest terms, the *I* resembles the Freudian ego[1] and the *Me* is self, the sense of inner life. As James (1892) put it: "Thoughts connected as we feel them to be connected are *what we mean* by personal selves" (pp. 153–154). Although the statement may not be scientifically valid, it is, nevertheless, what we mean.

James and Armstrong lead us toward a self with more dimensions than one defined through the concept of secrecy or the sense of innerness. First, there is the pole of awareness or consciousness, which is necessary to the experience. Second, other dimensions are suggested by the shape of inner life, which James compared with a bird's life, full of "flights and perchings" (p. 160). It does not go in straight lines. It is a capricious wandering thing, a flux of images, ideas, and memories linked by affect, analogy, and other associations. We return to the form of this experience later in the book, since its precursor is a certain kind of play. It is of interest in passing that Einstein compared his thinking processes during periods of creativity to play. He wrote:

> The words or the language, as they are written or spoken, do not seem to play any role in my mechanism of thought. The physical entities which seem to serve as elements in thought are certain signs and more or less clear images which can be "voluntarily" reproduced and combined. The above mentioned elements are, in my case, of visual and some of muscular type. Conventional words or other signs have to be sought for laboriously only in a secondary stage, when the mentioned associative play is sufficiently established and can be reproduced at will. [Hadamard 1945, pp. 142-143]

Einstein did not merely observe his thoughts. There is a sense of agency in his mental activity. The pole of consciousness that James had called the *I* moved the contents of consciousness about in an associative or combinatory play. A very important implication of this description is that consciousness is not merely passive, a simple searchlight, but active.

A third characteristic of our inner life is the sense of its movement. Although there is memory in it, the memories are not fixed, as if in their little boxes. Rather, there is an emancipation of memory in the present. James (1892) compared the feeling of constant change with the flow of a river. "No state once gone can recur and be identical with what was before" (p. 154). This sense of flow is often lost in those with disorders of self. The experience of stasis is accompanied by a diminished feeling of being alive. One of the results of successful therapy is the restoration of the feeling of flow. Anais Nin (1969) in the early phases of her treatment by Otto Rank, wrote, "Analysis is to do with flow . . . I am flowing again" (p. 214).

A fourth quality of inner life is its connectedness or unity. James (1892) declared that it "does not appear to itself chopped up in bits" (p. 154). Yet, such an experience, of being broken up in bits that do not connect, is an experience that those with borderline personality periodically suffer.

Finally, the experience of inner life goes in a kind of container, an inner space, which, of course, is not real space but a virtual space like that behind a mirror, which we perceive but know is not there. This space is not merely psychic; it includes the body. A body feeling and a background emotional state are with us all the time, although we may be barely aware of them (Meares 1980). They remain as a background emotional tone, which at its most basic is simply positive or negative—a vague state of well-being or an equally ill-defined sense of unease.

Experiences of the spatiality of self, of the body, and of the background emotional tone are all altered, in an episodic fashion, in those with disorders of self, fluctuating with the form of relationship with the social environment (Meares 1980). Anger, for example, closes one up. In contrast, in certain states of calm, there is a sense of opening up. These issues are discussed in more detail in later chapters.

We now consider the nature of the original doubleness out of which eventually arises the doubleness of inner life and, with it, the sense of self.

Chapter 4 | *I* AND THE OTHER

We are not born with a self. However, the I, or the ego, is neurophysiologically given. At birth we have a rudimentary ego, which matures as the central nervous system matures. The self, or the "me," is merely a possibility, a potentiality that will arise through an appropriate engagement of the child as "I" with the mother and other caregivers. The nature of this engagement must be the starting point of an attempt to understand how self develops.

The baby is born with the capacity to engage with others. This idea, that we possess innate, genetically encoded patterns or repertoires of behavior that are released by particular stimuli, seemed preposterous until the 1970s. Perhaps the most compelling evidence favoring the idea came from studies of birdsong. An intriguing example concerns the chaffinch. This bird sings in the springtime, but it is only the male that sings. However, if the female is given androgens, she too will sing. If the male is given androgens in a season other than springtime, he also sings. The hormone concentrates in an area in the midbrain. It is assumed that the trigger of the hormone releases a repertoire of the behavior of singing, which is intrinsic to the nervous system.[1]

Triggers of a similar kind operate in the development of the engagement between the baby and his or her caregivers. Patterns of reciprocal communicative behavior evolve between mother and baby that depend upon appropriate responses to cues or signals, often quite subtle, that both partners emit. To participate in this potential engagement, the baby must be perceptually competent. The extent of this competence surprised many when the results of the studies of the early 1970s began to emerge (Bower 1974).

What is striking about the newborn's abilities is his or her awareness of the stimuli that come from people, particularly the mother. For example, newborns turn toward a voice coming from behind a curtain, moving their head and hands as if searching for the speaker and in a way that shows some coordination. The newborn shows a preference for his or her own mother's voice. Her characteristic way of speaking seems to have been learned while the baby was in utero. Moreover, in the first few days the different syllables of speech, as well as their emotional tone, are discriminated by the baby (De Casper and Fifer 1980, Trevarthen 1987). The baby's ability to discriminate between mother and other people extends even to her smell—at about the age of 2 weeks, the baby prefers mother's breast pad to that of another woman (MacFarlane 1975). At about the same age, babies prefer to look at their own mothers' faces rather than the face of another woman, in this way appearing to show recognition of her (Carpenter 1974).

In addition to their unexpected ability to discriminate between such socially significant stimuli as voices and faces, babies behave in a way that encourages responses from others. Perhaps the most powerful trigger is the smile. Smiling occurs in blind children who could not mimic such behavior (McFarlane 1974). Babbling is also a characteristic of human infants.[2] More complex forms of communicative behavior may also be part of the infant's genetic endowment. These include patterns of sucking during feeding. The infant sucks in bursts, which are interspersed with pauses of about 4 to 15 seconds, during which he or she tends to gaze at mother's face (Brazelton et al. 1975). The mother's eyes are particularly important. The baby's smiling, babbling, pauses during feeding, and other subtler behaviors are triggers to a set of responses on the part of the mother. Maternal behaviors, which we suppose are also genetically evolved, are released by these stimuli.

The possibility that maternal behaviors, or parental behavior, is part of our evolutionary heritage is again supported by studies of animal behavior. In certain animals, the hormonal activation that occurs during the gestation and birth of a baby stimulates characteristic maternal repertoires of behavior that are presumably genetically encoded like the chaffinch song. For example, the pituitary hormone prolactin when injected into rats, whether they are male or female, causes them to begin to make nests.[3] Nothing so specific has been shown for humans. Nevertheless, characteristic maternal behaviors do seem to be triggered by the specific stimuli given off by the infant.

Klaus (1975) and others have described these behaviors. For example, at first contact with their babies after birth, mothers behave in a stereotyped way. They raise the pitch of their voices, show an intense interest in eye-to-eye contact, and tend to touch their babies first with fingertips to the extremities, then massaging the whole trunk and face.

THE PROTO-CONVERSATION

By the age of 2 months, the built-in behaviors of the mother and the child have meshed to a remarkable degree so that, in the 1970s, Trevarthen (1974) was able to describe what he called a *proto-conversation*. A reciprocal back-and-forward exchange between mother and baby is established, to which both contribute. Trevarthen (1983) describes the complex "dance" of the mother and the baby:

> In the second month infants become more precisely alert to the human voice and they exhibit subtle responses in expression to the flow of maternal speech. They are frequently content to engage in expressive exchanges for many minutes on end by means of sight and sounds alone . . . Definite eye contact is sought by most infants about 6 weeks after full term birth. Once this orientation is achieved, and in response to a complex array of maternal expressive signals, many 4-to-6-week-olds smile and coo . . . Mothers

align their faces with the baby, adjusting position to the least
distance of clear vision of an adult, and making modulated vertical
and horizontal head rotations. Their faces are exaggeratedly mobile
in every feature and these movements are synchronized with
gentle but rhythmically and accentuated vocalizations. All this
behavior responds to the infant's evident awareness and acts to
draw out signs of interest and pleasure. The infants show intent
interest with fixed gaze, knit brow and slightly pursed lips and
relaxed jaw, and immobility of the limbs. They exhibit an affec-
tionate pleasure, closely linked to fixation on the mother's face and
responsive to her expression, with smiles of varied intensity, coos,
and hand movements. [p. 139]

Trevarthen called this kind of engagement *primary intersubjectivity*. The behaviors of both partners are finely coordinated,
creating a shared structure of activity, which gives pleasure to
each but which neither could have generated alone.

When the proto-conversation was first described, some investigators doubted that it represented a true engagement. They
suggested that the apparent interaction was really a series of
reactions. This suggestion was difficult to counter using statistical
and mathematical methods. However, Trevarthen and his colleague, Lynne Murray (1985), devised a simple and very con-
vincing way of demonstrating that what was going on between
mother and baby was truly a shared structure of activity.

Mothers and their 6- to 12-week-old babies were placed in
separate rooms. The faces of each were televised and viewed by
the other partner in the other room. Each baby fully interacted
with his or her mother's image on the screen. Following this, the
image of mother was temporarily dislocated. The first minute of
interaction had been recorded and then replayed so that what the
baby now saw was the mother earlier in the interaction. Although
the baby was confronted by the same person whose face showed
the same affection and interest, the baby was distressed and
turned away.

The baby was distressed by a mismatching between the mother's response and the child's moment-to-moment experience. It
was as if the baby had an expectation of how the mother would
respond, and this was upset by the distortion of the image. The
mother usually acts in a way that is so sensitively attuned to the
baby's state that the baby may imagine the mother to be part of

his or her personal system, something like an extension of the baby's subjective life. When the mother does not act in this way, the baby is dismayed. In Kohut's (1971) terminology, the baby's conception of mother during this kind of interaction is not of an object who is a separate person, but of a *selfobject*, who is experienced as part of him or her, half of a single system made up of two major pieces.

Since the capacities of mother and child to make the engagement of the proto-conversation are genetically encoded, we might suppose that they have a neurophysiological basis. Our particular genetic endowments will provide us with nervous systems that differ in subtle ways. These biological differences might, conceivably, be reflected in different forms of mother–infant interaction. This possibility was investigated in a study of the form of an interaction of a series of mothers and their babies (Penman et al. 1983).

Each baby after birth was examined by methods developed by Brazelton and his colleagues (Als et al. 1977). The observations included the baby's orientation to social stimuli such as a face and a voice. These movements are presumed to be part of the innate neurophysiological capacities of the baby. Three months later, when the mother was not with her baby, she was tested in a room where a tone was periodically sounded. It had no particular meaning. Some mothers seemed fairly quickly to screen this irrelevant noise out of their consciousness since after a few soundings it excited no physiological reaction (in this case a fall in skin resistance). Other mothers, however, habituated much more slowly. These mothers, who showed more reactions to the noise, tended to have babies who showed relatively little social orientation. This type of mother–child pairing showed very rapid social cycling, that is, the periods of gazing at each other were relatively brief, being terminated by one or other of the partners averting his or her gaze. Following this, their mutual gaze would be restored to be once again quickly broken. In contrast, the pairing of mothers who habituated quickly and babies who showed clear social orientation produced a quite different form of interaction. This dyad characteristically gazed at each others' faces for long periods so that the cycles of gaze on/gaze off were slow.

We assumed that the different forms of interaction were normal for each pairing and that each partner was contributing to building up a pattern of interchange between the two that became characteristic of their engagement. We imagined a situation, however, in which the neurophysiology of mother did not match the baby so that she found it difficult to fit in with her child. Such an experience may be extremely upsetting for the mother, who may then assume that she is not cut out for motherhood or even that the baby does not like her. If such a situation persists, a chaotic dysynchrony between mother and child may arise, potentially disrupting development of self. It is helpful for these mothers to know that, in an important way, they are not to blame for the difficulty that, once its origin is realized, can be overcome.

MIRRORING

The mother's part in Trevarthen's proto-conversation and primary intersubjectivity is to provide a responsiveness that is attuned to the baby's state at that moment. This activity is often called *mirroring*, a term that is not quite accurate since it implies a simple reflecting back of the experience of the other. What the mother actually does is more complicated.

The role of vision in these early interactions is central. The baby and mother, or other caregiver, have their eyes fixed upon each other. The mother's gaze elicits responses from the baby, which the mother, in turn, responds to, often imitating something of the baby's expression. But this imitation is selective. The mother is much more likely to echo sounds that resemble the beginnings of language than nondescript crying noises. The mother is not simply a mirror. In her responsiveness to her infant, she gives back some part of what the baby is doing—but only some part and not all—and also gives him something of her own.

Kohut and Winnicott, in different ways, have emphasized the developmental significance of the mother's mirroring. Kohut focused on the mother's adoration of her infant—an idealization of the child that is represented in the religious imagery that lies at the heart of Western civilization. The joy in her baby that the mother feels is manifest on her face, showing the baby who she or he is. This leads us to the Winnicottian conception of the mother's face as a mirror. Winnicott (1974) asked: "What does the baby see when he or she looks at the mother's face? I am suggesting that, ordinarily, what the baby sees is himself or herself. In other words the mother is looking at the baby and *what she looks like is related to what she sees there"* (p. 131). As an example, a wriggling, excited infant, flailing his arms and kicking his legs as he lies on a bed, is looking up into a beaming face. This face shows him what he is—happy. And it evokes a further response in the baby. A kind of communication is going on that does not depend on words but on emotions and their expression. The baby expresses his affective state in his face, body, and vocalizations. The mother responds to these expressions in a way that mirrors them but also gives these emotions form. We may say, then, that affects are the coinage of the proto-conversation, the language of humanity before language eventually emerges, after a very considerable amount of development has occurred, during the second year of life.

This language of emotion, like the process of engagement, is part of our evolutionary endowment. In a classic study, Darwin (1872) showed that we share a variety of facial expressions with the higher animals. He suggested that these expressions, which register such emotions as joy, surprise, anger, fear, and disgust, are not simply conveyed to us by the mannerisms of a particular culture, but are part of our physiological makeup. The fact that these forms of expression are not culture bound has been confirmed by Izard (1971) and by Ekman and Friesen (1975).

Since the first form of engagement with another is so largely dependent on affect, which provides the "words" of the proto-conversation, we have an affective core (Emde 1983) to our lives that is shared by all humanity, so that, even in a foreign country, we are able to communicate, in a way. With those in our own social environment, we know that we are truly with another when the language of our discourse embraces emotional life. Affects are not only the words of the proto-conversation, they are central to those later relationships that we call intimate.

Chapter 5 | **THE ROLE OF TOYS**

The proto-conversation between the 2-month-old baby and the mother is between I and the other. There is no self in it. A third element needs to be found for self to evolve. This element is the world-to-be-manipulated.

In a baby's earliest days, nothing else is as interesting or entrancing while the mother is around. Soon, however, the baby begins to take an interest in the things around him or her. These things include clothes, bottles, parts of bodies, even the baby's voice, and, later, toys. The toys and other bits of the material world are now part of a triadic relationship with the mother and child. These things become the basis of self, or the *Me* in Jamesian terminology. It must be emphasized, however, that it is not the things alone that become the basis of self, but those things manipulated during an engagement of a particular kind with the mother and other caregivers.

The triadic relationship between the I, the selfobject, and the things is extraordinarily complex. Our studies of 3-month-old babies with their mothers and a small number of toys show that neither the baby's behavior nor the mother's is random (Penman et al. 1981). It is evident that the baby's interest in the toys is related to factors in his or her relationship with the mother. It cannot be conceived adequately as the child oscillating between two dyadic engagements of child–mother and child–toy. Rather, the mother participates in the child's play in a way that seems attuned to the infant's affect.

The Newsons, in Nottingham, England, have produced some charming video illustrations of what is essential to this behavior. For example, the mother is playing with soap bubbles. She blows these bubbles into the baby's face, where they burst. The baby is startled and does not know how to respond. The mother laughs, so the baby laughs too, knowing now that this is fun. It is as if the mother shapes, affectively, the baby's experience. She, by her attunement, gives it a kind of meaning. She mirrors it, if you like. It is tempting to believe that she could impose a reality, but in fact she cannot. If she laughs when it is inappropriate to do so, the baby becomes distressed.

The baby's behavior, when he or she looks into the mother's face for some signal concerning the meaning of a situation, has been studied by means of a modified visual cliff experiment (Sorce et al. 1985). The babies were a year old. As the children moved out over the transparent floor and saw space below them, they became apprehensive and looked toward their mothers. If the mother smiled and showed pleasure, the baby went on. If, however, the mother had been asked to show facial fear, the baby turned back, perhaps showing some distress.

The form of the tripartite engagement between I, the other, and things, which is the basis of play, changes with time. One striking feature concerns the child's increasing interest in the things. The findings of our study showed that at 3 months, only 12 percent of the baby's gaze was directed at the toys that were placed between the baby and the mother. The same mother–baby pairs were studied again at 6 months. At this age, 60 percent of the infants' gaze was directed at the toys (Penman et al. 1981). This increases further when the child begins to walk. Nevertheless, the pattern of turning to the caregiver for a response that gives meaning continues, particularly in explorative situations. For example, when children of 1 to 1½ years walk in a park with their mothers, they point at things while looking at her or bring them to her for inspection. Children in this situation "have been shown to bring and show adults [parent or observer] what they find interesting, and to do so often and continuously" (Garvey 1977, p. 51).

Soon, however, the trajectory of increasing interest in toys and play reaches the point where the child no longer seems to notice the parent. It was beautifully described by Piaget (1959) about half a century ago. The child chatters as he plays:

> What he says does not seem to him to be addressed to himself but is enveloped with the feeling of a presence, so that to speak of himself or to speak to his mother appear to him to be the same thing. His activity is thus bathed in an atmosphere of communion or syntonization, one might almost speak of "the life of union" to use the terms of mysticism, and this atmosphere excludes all consciousness of egocentrism. But, on the other hand, one cannot but be struck by the soliloquistic character of these same remarks. The child does not ask questions and expects no answer, neither does he attempt to give any definite information to his mother who is present. He does not ask himself whether she is listening or not. He speaks for himself just as an adult does when he speaks within himself. [p. 243]

The picture Piaget paints of the child at play is the basic scene of this book. It provides the principal metaphor upon which an approach to the evolution of self is built and also from which a theoretical framework for the treatment of disorders of self can be derived. Here is the embryonic self. To understand this notion, we must return to William James (1892), who had told us that "thoughts connected as we feel them to be connected are *what we mean* by personal selves" (pp. 153–154).

Although a flow of inner life may give adults a sense of existence, for infants this cannot be so. This is because, as we have already seen, the distinction between inner and outer worlds is not made, generally speaking, until the child is in the fifth year of life. The child who does not yet conceive of a boundary of self does not distinguish in a mature way between thoughts of things, which are inner, and those things themselves.[1] Rather, before the milestone of the private self is achieved, thoughts are mingled with, or even *in* the things. Thought cannot go on without them. For the child, then, things are necessary vehicles of a particular kind of thought, which is comparable with the flux of inner life in an adult.

For the adult, the inner life of images, ideas, and memories moves in the mind's eye against a space we know is not real space. It is a virtual space. It is as if inner experience is projected upon a metaphoric screen (Meares 1983). For the young child, the arena upon which thought is displayed, in toys, is real. In only a partly figurative way we can say that the play space is the precursor of inner space in adult life. It is where experiences are generated that become the core of what we mean by personal selves.

It must be emphasized that the whole scene is a precursor, including the enabling atmosphere provided by the parent. The eventual internalization of this scene includes a sense of the presence of the other. We now consider some of the characteristics of the play scene.

Chapter 6 | **TWO PLAYROOMS**

While the child is playing, he or she is generating a sense of what we mean by personal selves. This play, however, is of a particular kind. Play is a complex subject and includes many different kinds of activities that are typical of various ages. Piaget (1951) distinguished three main categories of play. The earliest he called *practice play*. It is presymbolic, involving activities such as banging a rattle, performed for the sake of pleasure. Play of older children is often social and involves rules. We are concerned with a form of play that falls between these two age groups. Piaget called it *symbolic play*. It goes on between the ages of approximately 1½ years and declines after the age of 4, that is, it occurs during that period of life before the individual has reached the stage of knowing an inner reality. The scene of symbolic play has several essential components that must be considered in some detail.

MAGIC AND REALITY

Symbolic play takes place in a curious atmosphere in which magic mingles with reality. Piaget (1929) pointed out that before the child conceives of a boundary to self, he lives in a largely personal universe in which his own mental life penetrates into his surroundings. This projection involves not only people, but also things. Flowers, clouds, the wind are given feelings and wishes that are similar to the child's, so that, for example, leaves wave in the breeze because they like it. The inanimate world is given the attributes of life.

Children's animism is paralleled by a magical omnipotence. Since the boundary between themselves and the outer world is limited, children believe that they and other people can exert undue influence upon it. For example, a 2½-year-old sways in front of a still pendulum, trying to make it swing. There is little gap between human wishes and their fulfillment. At this stage in human life, we believe we are immensely powerful. We believe that it is human activity that determines universal events. For example, a 4-year-old may believe that clouds move because we walk and that they obey us at a distance. An alternative explanation is animistic—because they are alive, they follow us. This sense of power is reinforced by the ordinary mother, behaving naturally, whose sensitivity to her infant's experience causes her to respond appropriately. For example, when the child is in discomfort, mother does something about it. It may be that the child believes that her mother's response was due to her own wish. In very early life when the objects of the infant's world have no enduring existence beyond her hearing or seeing them, the mother's comings and goings may be conceived as if the child has recreated her at each re-arrival. Although this magical system of thinking involves a sense of power, it also has its terrors. The child not only is able to recreate the mother, but also is able to cause the mother to vanish.

Remnants of magical ways of thinking are found in adult life and are manifest in all cultures, for example, in such practices as rain-making rituals or sticking pins into images of enemies in order to harm them. Nevertheless, this kind of thinking has a particular immediacy in early childhood, making play exciting, and even frightening.

The world of play, however, is not only magical, but also real. The child uses physical objects, bits of the material world, as the elements of play. That these things are real is as important as the fact that they are vehicles of imagination, as Winnicott (1953) pointed out in his classic description of the centerpiece of much of the child's play—the transitional object. Winnicott's concept must be discussed briefly since it is fundamental.

The transitional object is the child's special possession—a doll, a teddy bear, a blanket, or something similar that is soothing, especially when the parents are not around. In the sense that aspects of the mothering function adhere to it, the transitional object symbolizes the mother. But that is not all it does. Aspects of the child's self are projected onto it, as if it were an extension of his or her own reality. The little boy or girl, from time to time, chatters to the doll or teddy bear. It is as if the child talks to himself and, at the same time, to someone else. In this situation the doll or teddy bear performs functions that it cannot have in reality. It is an illusion. But it is also real. Winnicott emphasizes the importance of the paradox that the same thing is both actual and an illusion.

A final and cardinal characteristic of the transitional object is that it is owned. Nobody in the family will dispute the fact that this object is the child's possession. The child's ownership of it provides a first step toward the sense of ownership of an internal world.

SELFOBJECT

Play goes on in a space in which there is neither inner nor outer and in which internal reality and external reality coexist. It cannot go on, however, if the child feels that he or she is alone.

As the child plays and chatters, he seems to be talking to himself, or else as if there were little distinction between his thoughts and those of the mother. To the objective observer, the mother is being ignored. However, the awareness of the mother penetrates into the intimacy of every wish and thought. The child experiences her as an extension of his own personal world. Piaget (1959) uses the phrase *the life of union* to describe that state when the other is conceived as an extension of subjective life, as part of the child's self-system rather than an object in relation to subject. This experience of the other as selfobject, as Kohut called it, is necessary for play to begin and to be maintained.

The enabling climate provided by the other is not merely

passive. The mother is not simply present if play is to go on. She must be attentive and responsive. Yet, at the same time, as in Piaget's description, she is not salient or intrusive. Rather, she fits in with the child's experience so that she becomes the atmosphere of it. A study of Sorce and Emde[1] is consistent with this idea. They showed in a study of 15-month-old children that the mother's emotional availability is essential to play. When the mother was not available (in this case she was reading the newspaper), the effects in play were striking. The infants were subdued, were less explorative, and stayed closer to their mothers. Their play was less advanced in that it tended to consist of passively touching or holding toys, without using them in ways that were functionally appropriate (e.g., stacking nesting cups) or thematically appropriate (e.g., pretending to talk on the telephone).

The concept of the selfobject is Kohut's greatest contribution to our understanding of psychological development. Like the transitional object, it can be described simply, yet it is a complex idea. For example, the way in which the parent will function as selfobject will differ according to age. The mother who the 3-year-old seems to ignore while playing is behaving very differently from the mother in Trevarthen's proto-conversation. She, too, is conceived as an extension of the infant's self system, but she is clearly salient and active. Nevertheless, she fits in with the infant's needs.

The theory of the selfobject involves subtleties that are still being explored. They include the following question: Is the selfobject an actuality, a real person, or is it a construction of the infant, and so not real? One difficulty of deciding between these alternatives is that the authoritative accounts of the selfobject came from clinicians' observations of their relationships with those with personality disorders rather than from descriptions of children. The experience of the other as an extension of self in the clinical situation may differ from that of infancy. Nevertheless, these clinical accounts are valuable. Kohut's is the most significant.

In his work with a 25-year-old woman, Miss F., Kohut was struck by the way she responded to him. First, she could not tolerate his silence, nor would noncommittal remarks satisfy her. After he had remained silent for a considerable period, she would suddenly become violently angry. He learned, however, that she would quickly become calm when, in essence, he restated what she had been saying. Second, he learned that he could not go beyond this restatement and attempt, say, to impose his perception of meaning upon what she had been saying. Kohut described her response. She ". . . would furiously accuse me, in a tense, high-pitched voice, of undermining her; that with my remark, I had destroyed everything she had built up; that I was wrecking the analysis" (p. 286).

We might suppose that he had invaded an experience that was analogous to play. He broke it up by attempting to bring into it aspects of a reality that came from outside. Kohut began to realize that she needed him to ". . . be nothing more than the embodiment of a psychological function which the patient's psyche could not yet perform for itself; to respond enthusiastically to her narcissistic sustenance through approval, mirroring and echoing" (p. 287). Put another way, she needed him to function as a selfobject.

Some authoritative definitions of the selfobject stress Kohut's notion of function. For example, Stolorow (1986) maintains that "the term *selfobject* does not refer to environmental entities or care-giving agents—that is, to people. Rather, it designates a class of psychological *functions* pertaining to the maintenance, restoration and transformation of self-experience" (p. 389).

The idea of the selfobject as an almost disembodied set of functions contrasts with an alternative set of descriptions that recognizes that the selfobject is actually a person. Lichtenberg (1983), for example, states that "selfobjects refer to aspects of caregivers—mother, father, teachers, etc.—who are experienced as providing something necessary for the maintenance of a stable, positively toned self sense of self" (p. 166). Goldberg (1988) is another who sees the selfobject as a "*person* (italics added) who is experienced as performing a necessary psychic function for the self" (p. 204).

We have, then, two viewpoints. One view is of the caregiver, perhaps the mother, who is a real person acting in a particular way. The other is of an experience that is almost illusory. The selfobject according to Wolf (1988), "is neither self nor object, but the *subjective* aspect of a self-sustaining function performed by a relationship of self to objects who by their presence or activity evoke and maintain the self and the experience of selfhood" (p. 184). My resolution of this apparent conflict is this. Both viewpoints are right and fundamental. It is necessary, at least in terms of the field of play, that the other is both real and illusory *at the same time*. The simultaneous experience of reality and illusion links the selfobject to the transitional object. They are parallel and related concepts. Although they are linked and have some similar properties, they must not coalesce. Where the mother becomes the transitional object, difficulties arise in the child's development. This may be manifest in problems with aloneness that arise in the following way.

We have seen so far that the particular form of mental activity manifest in play needs the enabling atmosphere provided by a caregiver who is responding in a certain way. However, children play when there is nobody actually present, for example, in their own rooms. We suppose, however, that in this setting there is a sense of the presence of the other that the physical surroundings provide. The child will also play in less familiar surroundings. What helps to provide the requisite atmosphere in these circumstances is often the transitional object. Where the mother does not allow this situation to develop, but continues, for example, to soothe her child at every opportunity, her functions cannot eventually be transferred to the child. The child's "capacity to be alone" (Winnicott 1958) is preceded by periods during earlier development when he or she acts as if alone in the presence of the other. The progression to the stage where the other can be away for long periods is impeded if the mother or other caregiver takes on the role of transitional object. Where this occurs, the child's going-on-being depends upon the actual presence of the selfobject, and psychic life is not experienced as "owned."[2]

IDEALIZATION AND GRANDNESS

The scene of play has a particular affective quality. Piaget's description of the child at play implies an activity of great pleasure. It suggests a particular feeling tone that is difficult to describe. The feeling tone gives a value to these experiences, which are the primary atoms of the evolving constellation of self.

The feeling tone, however, is not confined to the child. The whole scene is imbued with this experience so that, together with the child, the person whose presence has created this atmosphere is ideal.

Coupled with the sense of idealization is an awareness of power, not only of the omnipotent child, but of the other who creates the enabling environment. Indeed, this person is conceived, so Piaget's anecdotes would lead us to believe, as if he or she has created the child's experience or, at least, contributed to its making. "The small child receives from the adult the double impression of being dominated by a mind far superior to his own and at the same time of being completely understood by this mind with which he shares everything" (Piaget 1959, p. 244). Nevertheless, he conceives her as part of himself so that at times he reacts toward her "as a glorified omnipotent alter ego" (p. 257). Indeed, because of a limited conception of boundary between them, there are times when she is he, and he is she. Their relations are reversible. When he feels and acts the way he perceives her to be, he becomes like her. He is grand. The child's experience, then, is bipolar, one pole being associated with well-being and goodness, the other with power.

This notion of the bipolar self was introduced by Baldwin nearly a century ago.[3] It was taken up by Kohut and elaborated, in a different way, as a central part of this theory. Kohut (1977) called the two poles *idealizing* and *grandiose.* Since the aim of therapy with those with personality disorder is to help the developmental process begin again at the point where it has been derailed or stifled, these two poles of experience almost inevitably emerge as part of a successful therapeutic encounter.

INNERNESS AND LANGUAGE

The playing child is absorbed in the activity like an adult who is lost in thought. This observation leads to the form of the child's language when playing.

A cardinal feature of the preschool child's play is an embryonic innerness. This is evident in the child's language. Piaget (1959) gives an example of a little boy, age 3, who is drawing in the presence of an adult. "There, I'm drawing in this sheet. I'm making a funny man. What am I doing? It's a waterworks. Here

I must draw the water. Now the water. I'll make a boat too. A little boat and an Indian, a man and woman, two men and a woman. Two men and an Indian. They've fallen in the water, you see" (p. 242). The *you* to whom he speaks and whom he questions is himself. "He speaks for himself just as an adult does when he speaks within himself" (p. 243).

This emergent innerness is an immediate precursor to that stage of experience that is maturely inner, when one's thoughts are truly one's own. The language used is not for communication with others or for adaptive purposes. Rather, *it seems necessary to the representation of a personal reality.*

The language of the playing child has a peculiar form. It shows abbreviations, it jumps, and it is not grammatical. It moves by analogy, resemblance, and other associations. An older child does not talk in this way. Piaget had assumed that, with maturation, this form of language, which he called egocentric since it was not designed to communicate, simply atrophies and disappears. The Russian psychologist Vygotsky, however, came to a very different, and in terms of this discussion, very important view.

In brief, Vygotsky (1962) argued that the egocentric monologue does not vanish. Rather, it is internalized to become inner speech. It has quite a different structure than socialized speech. It is not "speech minus sound," but is an "entirely separate speech function. Its main distinguishing trait is its peculiar syntax. Compared with external speech, inner speech appears disconnected and incomplete" (pp. 138–139). It is to a large extent "thinking in pure meanings. It is a dynamic, shifting, unstable thing, fluttering between word and thought" (p. 49). This resemblance depends upon a "basic semantic peculiarity of inner speech—the way in which senses of words combine and unite—a process governed by different laws from those governing combinations of meanings" (p. 147). Vygotsky called this singular way of uniting words an *influx of sense.* "The senses of different words flow into one another—literally 'influence' one another—so that the earlier ones are contained in, and modify, the later ones" (p. 147). This is a process very like the condensation that, as Freud had pointed out, is characteristic of dreams. In a less specific, somewhat poetic way, Winnicott repeatedly remarked upon the similarities between playing and dreaming.

THE "REAL" PLAYROOM

The room or other space in which play goes on has qualities that are beyond the physical facts of the floor, the windows, the toys. The other's presence as selfobject and the embryonic experience of innerness create an atmosphere that is not only real but also illusory. At times, however, the child inhabits a playroom that is entirely real.

From time to time the child's play is interrupted by events around him, which alert him. What alerts him may include any of the myriad events in ordinary living, or changes in the enabling atmosphere provided by the other. He orients now toward the external world. The field of play is broken and play stops. Of course, this is part of normal development. A different kind of engagement now occurs. The other person is now an object, no longer a selfobject. The child's language and concerns are clearly adaptive. He asks for things, inquires, and responds. His experience at this point has lost whatever was inner in the play. His attention is directed entirely outward. His language is linear, logical, and directed toward reality. It has the form of what Freud called *secondary process*. This space is real. Here is generated the core of the *social me*, as James called it. The child switches back and forth between these two modes of engagement with the nurturing environment, often very quickly. Kohut (1984) has distinguished these two kinds of engagement as between two experiences of the "you." In the first case, the "you" functions as a selfobject; in the second as an object. Put another way, we may say that the child's experience oscillates between two spaces, one of which is totally real and the other both real and unreal (or perhaps imagined or illusory). Both experiences are necessary to proper maturation, but one is very much more fragile than the other. The life of union in which the other is a selfobject is interrupted not only by the ordinary circumstances of living, but also by failures of parental attunement, as noted in a later chapter. Where family life is chaotic and intrusive—a large number of borderline personalities have been victims of sexual or physical abuse[4]—and where parental failure of attunement becomes chronic, the play space is never adequately or securely established and the child is relatively deprived of circumstances in which might be generated the core experiences of what we mean by personal selves. The child is left with a sense of no real "me" and an orientation and dependence upon outer reality. Seen in this way, the fragile play space becomes the basic metaphor that underlies the treatment of those with disorders of self.

In summary, the child alternates between two kinds of experiences that go on in different spaces. Much of the time, the child is oriented to the outer environment, adapting to others and coping with the world. In play, however, there is no adaptation to reality. On the contrary, I am supposing, the child takes pieces of the external world and uses them in play to represent, and so to bring into being, a personal reality.

FRAGMENTS OF SPACE
Chapter 7 | AND OF SELF

In the previous chapter we found the child living, alternately, in one of two spaces. The child of 2 or 3 cannot live in both at the same time. Subtle differences in affect and more profound differences in attention and language show that, in a sense, he or she is a different person in each space. Seen in this way, the child's existence is discontinuous. Such discontinuity is hard to imagine in adult life. Nevertheless, in minor forms, the experience is not uncommon, particularly in young people. For example, Paul Klee (1964) describes himself at the age of 22 as if he were an actor in a series of roles:

> My self, for instance, is a dramatic ensemble. Here a prophetic ancestor makes his appearance. Here a brutal hero shouts. Here an alcoholic *bon vivant* argues with a learned professor. Here a lyric muse, chronically lovestruck, raises her eyes to heaven. Here papa steps forward, uttering pedantic protests. Here the indulgent uncle intercedes. Here the aunt babbles gossip. Here the maid giggles lasciviously. And I look upon it all with amazement, the sharpened

pen in my left hand. A pregnant mother wants to join the fun. "Pshtt!" I cry, "You don't belong here. You are divisible." And she fades out. [p. 177]

An extreme illustration of discontinuity in the adult is provided by the phenomenon of the multiple personality, who switches between more or less discrete constellations of character traits. Memory, to a significant degree, remains compartmentalized, so that a particular personality only has access to the past experiences of that personality. For the child, discontinuity is a feature of early development. In this chapter, the subject is considered first in terms of the implications of the two playrooms and then from the more general point of view of the multiplicity of selves in early development.

SELF AND THE SOCIAL ME

The play of the kind that is the focus of this book does not take place before about 18 months of age, since it involves language. The child in Piaget's ideal scene is chattering to him- or herself. By the age of 18 months, the child has a vocabulary of about two dozen words. Six months later, the child's lexicon is about ten times greater, so that a child of 2 may know 250 to 300 words (Anisfeldt 1984). It is clear that around 18 months an enormous change occurs in the child's development. For the first time, the child comes to recognize him- or herself as an individual with identifying characteristics that give him or her a particular place in a social system. Put another way, the *social me* emerges. During the same period, a self is being created in episodes of absorption in play.

The beginnings of the child's behavior as a social being are shown in a number of ways. The first, of course, is language. As we have seen, however, words are the means not only of communication with others, but also of representing a personal reality.

The body also comes to be recognized in its social sense. At about 18 months, the child begins to show evidence of recognition of his or her mirror image, that is, the child comes to see him- or herself as others do.[1] This is inferred from observations of children's behavior when they see themselves in a mirror. When a rouge mark has been surreptitiously placed on the child's nose, the child of about 18 months and older tries to rub it off. He or she shows that "this mark is not me." At the same time, the child shows by actions that "I know this is me I am looking at." Although children who are younger than about 18 months do not seem to recognize their own image, they have nevertheless stored and integrated a great deal of complex information about the body that is not social but purely personal. For example, there is evidence that babies of 3 to 8 months have a quite complex body schema derived from internal sensation coming from such sources as muscle and joint. Children of this age can make suitable adjustments of their bodies when placed in a room where visual cues indicate that the room is tilted (Lewis 1990). This finding suggests that there is a large amount of information to which small children have access and use, but of which they are not conscious.

Fluctuations in body feeling are part of the inner awareness of self. They usually connect, often in a subtle way, with outer manifestations of the same state, such as facial expression and bodily movement. In most cases, we find a harmony between the inner sense of the body and what is shown socially. As we see in a later chapter, however, in disorders of self, there is often a dislocation between the persona (Jung 1953), which is the mask shown to the world, and more personal experience. The persona, the outwardly displayed aspect of the person one is in relation to others, is elaborated to a substantial degree between 18 months and 4 years of age. This evolution is shown in gender identity, which involves the adoption of a certain appearance created by hair style, dress, manners of speech, and motor activity. From these rather obvious features extend a range of subtler behaviors to do with characteristic forms of emotional expression and interpersonal transactions. These have become so developed by the age of 4 that a child brought up in a role conflicting with his or her chromosomal gender has difficulty in changing (Money and Ehrhardt 1972).

Language and the persona are not the only changes in the child's life that show emergence as a social being. Michael Lewis has pointed out that emotions related to social life begin to be expressed following the first awareness of one's image as it appears to others. Although anger can be demonstrated at 2 months and anxiety at 6 months, emotions that modify and influence our social relationships do not become manifest until much later. Self-conscious emotions such as coyness and embarrassment appear during the second half of the second year of life (Lewis and Brooks-Gunn 1979). Other socially significant emotions such as pride, shame, and guilt begin to be displayed between 24 and 30 months (Lewis 1990, 1992). However, just as language and the body cannot be seen as entirely to do with the social world, these social emotions are also related to self. Shame, for example, is the result of exposure of something felt to be intensely personal.

In summary, then, a range of developments in language, bodily awareness, and emotional expression show that great change occurs in the child's life during the second half of the second year. In essence, they indicate the emergence of a social "me" that is related to, but can be distinguished from, an embryonic self.

BEFORE SIX MONTHS

During the second half of the second year, the social me and the self are beginning to evolve in different experiential spaces. The idea that experiences have locations leads to the proposition that experiences create or constitute the spaces in which they occur. This proposal implies that early in life, personal space will be multiple. In the beginning, we suppose "there is a juxtaposition of different and local spaces without intercoordination: a mouth space, a visual space, a tactile space, a postural space, and so on" (Gruber and Vonèche 1977, p. 219). This fragmentation of personal existence can be inferred from studies such as those of Spitz.

In a famous series of observations, Rene Spitz (1965) seemed to show that for the baby, the world is in bits. He recorded the child's response to a mask. A baby of 2 months will smile at a mask with eyes but no mouth, or a scowling mouth. At a slightly later age, a congruent mouth is needed to produce a smile, but a profile excites no response. A somewhat older baby smiles at the profile. It is as if the child perceives pieces of the environment that are at first quite small, like eyes, lips, and nose, but with development is able to integrate them into large coherences.

The discontinuity of early experience can also be inferred from studies of memory. The evidence suggests that in the first few months, the infant has a recognition memory but has no capacity for spontaneous recall.[2] As a result, the reality of the small baby is entirely constituted by experiences in the present. The baby does not conjure up images and feelings associated with those who are absent. All that it knows is happening now. Reality, to a large extent, consists of others and is consequently broken up by the comings and goings of various caregivers.

Since these comings and goings concern different experiences, they occur in different spaces. A corollary to the original proposition now emerges. Not only do experiences constitute spaces, but spaces determine the existence of the experiences and the objects that are part of them. Each object and each experience has its own place, and this place identifies it. When the object moves from that place, it is no longer the same object and ceases to exist. Piaget (1954) came across the idea in playing with his small daughter while she was sitting in bed.

> Jacqueline tries to grasp a celluloid duck on top of her quilt. She almost catches it, shakes herself, and the duck slides down beside her. It falls very close to her hand but behind a fold in the sheet. Jacqueline's eyes have followed the movement, she has even followed it with her outstretched hand. But as soon as the duck has disappeared—nothing more! It does not occur to her to search behind the fold of the sheet, which would be very easy to do (she twists it mechanically without searching at all) . . . I then take the duck from its hiding place and place it near her hand three times. All three times she tries to grasp it, but when she is about to touch it I replace it very obviously under the sheet. Jacqueline immediately withdraws her hand and gives up. The second and third times I make her grasp the duck through the sheet and she shakes it for a brief moment but it does not occur to her to raise the cloth. [pp. 36–37]

Jacqueline's behavior is characteristic of a child of 4 to 5 months. She acts as if the object has no enduring existence after it disappears. Her behavior suggests that she conceives a personal universe that is not only in pieces, but constantly shifting. Since the disappearance of the object from its space means it ceases to exist, its reappearance is a manifestation of its re-creation. Thus objects have only a precarious permanence. The child believes that the things are ceaselessly being made and unmade. Furthermore, since the object constitutes the space in which it was experienced, the vanishing object leads to a dissolution of that experiential space. "The notion of space at this stage is fragmentary since objects dissolve into nothingness" (Gruber and Vonèche 1977, p. 219).

SIX MONTHS TO 18 MONTHS

The experiental world of the infant is, as it were, fragmented. There seems to be a multiplicity of objects when only a few are there. The idea that the position of an object in space is an essential part of its existence suggests that the child's environment is filled with objects such as ball-under-the-armchair, doll-attached-to-the-hammock, mother-at-the-window. Should the ball roll under a sofa, it becomes a different object—ball-under-the-sofa. If mother moves, she becomes mother-at-the-fireplace. It is as if the world were like a cinematic film that had been broken down into its individual frames. The child of, say, 4 months conceives a single other as multiple. Thus the concept of mother is made up of a parade of many women, all of them recognizable but not directly connected. This somewhat outlandish hypothesis seems, at first sight, difficult to test. Nevertheless, the ingenious Scottish psychologist, Tom Bower (1971), has conducted an experiment that does just this. He described it in the following way:

> I shall describe infants who sat in front of an arrangement of mirrors that produced two or three images of a person. In some instances the infant was presented with two or three images of his mother; in others he would see his mother and one or two strangers who were seated so that they were in a position identical with the earlier additional images of his mother.
>
> In the multiple-mother presentation, infants, less than 20 weeks old, happily responded with smiles, coos and arm-waving to each mother in turn. In the mother-stranger presentation the infants

were also quite happy and interacted with their mother as one of many identical mothers. They do not recognize the identity of the multiple mothers in the special sense in which I have used the word "identity," that is, they do not identify the multiple images of the mother, as belonging to one and the same person.

Infants more than 20 weeks old also ignored the stranger and interacted with their mothers. In the multiple-mother situation, however, the older infants became quite upset at the sight of more than one mother. This shows, I would argue, that the younger infants do identify objects with places and hence think they have a multiplicity of mothers. Because the older infants identify objects by features, they know they have only one mother, and this is why they are upset by the sight of multiple mothers. [p. 30]

Bower's experiment suggests that around 6 months a considerable integration of the concept of mother has occurred. This change is paralleled by a difference in the way the child behaves with physical objects. At about 6 months, the child no longer seems to think that an object is the same object as long as it is in the same place and that all objects in the same place are the same object. Nevertheless, object permanence—the infant's apparent certainty that an object continues to exist despite its disappearance—is not fully achieved until 18 months.

The integration of the concept of mother and other caregivers that occurs at about 6 to 7 months is paralleled by some unification of the concept (or representation) of self. This assumption depends upon the idea that for the baby every experience of the other is linked to an experience of him- or herself. During the period of development when *mother* refers to a range of disconnected experiences, the baby's own experience consists of a similar and related range of multiple selves. If the concept of the other is unified, to some extent at least, by about 6 to 7 months, we should expect a similar coalescence in the concept of self. This, again, is not an easy hypothesis to test. Nevertheless, Michael Lewis suggested a way to do it.

Lewis and Brooks (1978) remark that by 6 to 8 months, infants begin to realize objects have an existence of their own. "If an infant knows that objects exist, he must also know he exists separate from the objects. It would be reasonable to assume that knowledge of others, self and objects develop at the same time" (p. 211). Lewis uses this idea to explain the emergence of anxiety at 7 to 8 months. If anxiety arises as a response to a threat to the integrity of self, then it can only arise when the baby has some sense of himself as an entity and some ability to evaluate a threat to this entity. This argument gains support from observations of children who were observed on the visual cliff. Children of 5 and 9 months of age crawled out over a glass flooring, seeing a space emerge below them. Both groups of children had their heart rates recorded while they did this. The younger group was quite aware of what was happening but seemed interested rather than alarmed. This was indicated by a drop in heart rate. The older babies' heart rates rose, an index of fear (Schwartz et al. 1973). Thus the older children apparently sensed a threat to their existence, whereas the younger ones did not.

The entity that is self at 6 to 7 months is a preliminary and relative one. This can be inferred from the child's behavior with objects. If we follow the idea that knowledge of others, self, and objects develops at the same time, we suppose that how the child of a particular age conceives of physical objects will be related to, and will throw some light on, the child's concept of self at the same age. Evidence suggests that infants younger than 18 months continue to display a residual tendency to identify objects with places (Bower 1974). Accordingly, we infer that a discontinuity of personal existence persists, at least to 1½ years. Piaget (1954) gives an example of this residual tendency. He describes Gerard, aged 13 months, who is playing ball in a large room.

> The ball rolls under an armchair. Gerard sees it and not without some difficulty takes it out in order to resume the game. Then the ball rolls under a sofa at the other end of the room. Gerard has seen it pass under the fringe of the sofa, he bends down to recover it. But as the sofa is deeper than the armchair and the fringe does prevent a clear view, Gerard gives up after a moment; he gets up, crosses the room, goes right under the armchair and carefully explores the place where the ball was before. [p. 59]

Children a little older than Gerard no longer search for a hidden object in a place where it was previously found. They cannot cope, however, with invisible displacements of the object in space (Bower 1974). At 18 months, this difficulty is also overcome. At this stage the child acts as if objects have a stable existence whether visible or not.

CULTURAL SPACE

This child's conception of the permanence of objects has important implications for the stability of personal existence. During the period leading up to 18 months, we assume that the personal experience of the child has a somewhat shifting and fragmented quality. With the attainment of object permanence at about 18 months comes the idea that the space in which things are is relatively stable and enduring. The play space, then, is also relatively enduring so that experiences going on within it, which are the beginnings of self, have a certain stability.

This zone of experience is embryonically inner—the region of self. At 18 months, the child also enters a second zone of experience, which is outer and particularly social. Out of it develops, over many years, an individual identity. Until about the age of 4, the potentially inner zone is both inner and outer. It is transitional, in Winnicott's language. With the attainment of the concept of boundary of self, the two zones become, in theoretical terms, quite distinct, and inner space is formed. Whereas the scene in transitional space is actual and visible, the view upon this new location of a personal reality is metaphoric, no longer dependent upon things.

The attainment of the sense of an inner world brings with it something else. By the age of about 5, the child not only distinguishes two main zones of personal experience, but also that inner and outer should connect. Consider the following story told by a 6-year-old:

> Once there was a child. He was very wild. His name was Kind. Every single person thought it was a terrible name for a wild person. One day when Kind was playing, he saw a little girl. She was crying, so Kind went to the little girl. The little girl said, "Find a little doll for me."
> Kind said, "No, I will not."
> "You are not Kind to me," said the little girl.
> Kind began to cry and said, "I will never be unkind again."

The author of this little story seems to conceive an essential reality of the boy, which is known only to himself and which is indicated by his name. His identity, or social me, is different. The little girl's response makes him realize the disconnection between the two zones of experience. People with disorders of self also experience a sense of desolation on becoming aware that they live in two separate domains and that the gulf between them seems un-bridgeable.

How the connection between these two zones is achieved is a mystery few writers have pondered. Winnicott is one of those who have explored the area. He began his inquiry by acknowl-edging two kinds of experience, one of which is found in contemplation, the other in the outer world where we exist simply in terms of behaviors. As Winnicott pointed out, however, we do not spend most of our lives either lost in contemplation or as pure extroverts. A third concept is required. In my view, this is not created until the concept of privacy is attained and a boundary to self is conceived of. Using Winnicott's language, this experiential area might be called *cultural space*. The child's rela-tionship with others is now changed and considerably more complex.

Consider the following extract from one of the children in our privacy study.

Girl (5.2 years):
 What are Cathy and Paul doing?
 Don't know.
 Are they playing?
 Playing a game.
 How do they play?
 She tells him a secret.
 What's a secret?
 I don't know any, but I can make up one.
 Make up one, then!
 Um (whispers). *We're going to the beach tomorrow, we'll build a*
  sandcastle, and when we knock it down, guess what's inside?
 Do I have to guess?
 Yes!
 Shells?
 No.
 Goggles and flippers?
 No!
 Surfboard? Egg?
 No! No!

I give up!
Promise you won't tell?
Yes.
Inside the sandcastle is a princess!
Can I tell anyone at all?
No!
If you could tell one person, who would it be?
No one!
Can I tell your mummy?
No nobody AT ALL!

This little girl is showing an extraordinary complexity of mental operations. First, she lives in the public or social domain. She plays a game with the interviewer, acting out the essentials of the concept of secrecy in her whispering and in her command that what she tells must not be revealed. She also draws on private experience where she conjures up the image of the beach and the hidden princess, who, perhaps, is part of a larger fantasy that concerns herself. The child coordinates the public and private domains so that they are unified and seamlessly connected.

There is also an exchange between them. As noted in Chapter 2, the emergence of the concept of the self-boundary and the consequent discovery of cultural space brings with it a profound change in relating to others. In contrast to the child absorbed in symbolic play, who appears to be ignoring others and whose activity involves no interchange, the more mature child is now able to engage in a reciprocal form of relationship. It involves choice. The child is free to reveal, or not to reveal, something of a world that is private and personal. The act of showing another that which is usually secret has the effect of an offer, inviting a similar act in return. This manner of interrelating is a fundamental aspect of intimacy.

The child's new knowledge of the concept of exchange is reflected in play. After the age of 4, games with rules begin to be played. Such games, which are more clearly seen after 7 years of age (Piaget, 1951), involve not only alliances and exchanges, but also combat, agreement, and other transactions. In contrast, the play of the child in the transitional period has no rules except that the things with which the child plays must be recognized as his or her own.

The story of the princess and the sandcastle shows that the

child has acquired the means of linking frames of experience beyond the public and private. To these domains are linked those of present and future. As she plays out the secret in the present, she also projects it into the future "on the beach tomorrow." She displays a remarkable unification of various dimensions of existence. With this unity comes a sense of duration, a personal continuity.

To conclude, this chapter concerns the spatiality of self. In the beginning of life, self is discontinuous, this experience going on as if in multiple places. By 18 months, considerable integration has occurred so that the child's existence is in two main spaces. One of these is the public domain where the individual's identity emerges. The second space is both public and private—the play space—in which is generated an embryonic self. By about 4 years of age, the play space becomes private. A new way of relating to others evolves in which private and public zones of experience are coordinated. With this milestone arises not only a further sense of coherence and unity of self, but also an enhanced awareness of temporality and personal continuity.

Chapter 8 | FIT AND SELF-ESTEEM

The play space is constituted by a sense of the presence of another who is experienced as an extension of the child's personal world. The responsiveness of this other person, the selfobject, *fits* with the child's immediate states of feeling and imagining. In this chapter, I suggest that responses from others who fit an evolving personal reality have an effect, often quite subtle, of evoking a positive emotional tone, a state of well-being of which the individual is usually only dimly aware. An accumulation of these moments leads to a relatively enduring positive feeling about oneself. Put another way, it leads to the growth of self-esteem. Those with disorders of self are left with the opposite condition—a persisting feeling of dysphoria and of personal worthlessness. This low self-esteem is often concretized as feelings of badness, incompetence, even ugliness.

Before considering the background to a hypothesis about the development of self-esteem, it is necessary to confront a possible difficulty in conceiving self. In the previous paragraph the term *self* is implicitly used in two different ways. First, self refers to one's immediate moment-by-moment sense of existence. Second, it also refers to an enduring constellation of the experiences. This second usage, which conceives of self as an organized structure of memories of states of personal existence, is *self-representation* (Jacobson 1964). Self-esteem is part of this structure.

Despite our intuitive feeling that we know what it is and how it might arise, self-esteem is not well understood. The results of the large amount of research in the area have been disappointing,[1] presumably because the subject has a somewhat intangible quality, difficult to define. P. Robson (1988) points out that influential definitions of the term are discrepant, often apparently describing different entities. Indeed, his view is at odds with my own, so illustrating the difficulties of the subject. Robson believes that quite clearly, self-esteem is an idea, whereas the main thesis of this chapter is that it is based on feeling.

Attempts to conceptualize self-esteem in purely social or behavioral terms have not been particularly successful. The most famous of these attempts came from William James.

William James (1892, p. 187) formulated self-esteem in a way that related it to identity rather than self. His well-known equation

$$\text{self-esteem} = \frac{\text{success}}{\text{pretensions}}$$

can be seen as the origin of much research into the subject. This equation suggests that achievement is necessary to self-esteem. However, our everyday experience upsets this simple idea. A man whose life might seem to other eyes to be miserable and fruitless, has a humor and quiet confidence that shows that circumstances have not diminished him. In contrast, another man whose achievements have been outstanding may consider himself a failure.

A further puzzle about self-esteem is that those in whom it is low do not all come from families or a social environment in which they have been excessively criticized or denigrated. Although it is obvious that such an atmosphere cannot be useful in helping developing people to feel positive about themselves, it may not be the most fundamental mechanism for the production of low self-esteem. After all, a person's central feelings about him- or herself are likely to be found in interpersonal experiences that are earlier than those that depend on the use of language. We need to discover a source more primitive and archaic than the congruence, or lack of it, between an individual's aspirations and their actual fulfillment. The Jamesian equation does not help us understand the more basic and fundamental self-esteem that is growing before pretensions are recognized. Indeed, the Jamesian approach may underlie the almost conscious strivings of those in whom success is used in an attempt to overcome a basic feeling of low self-esteem.

A further difficulty about the Jamesian equation, and of research implicitly based upon it, concerns affect. Self-esteem is not simply a response to a rational matching between, say, goals and achievement. Such cold considerations leave out the difficult-to-describe feeling of well-being that is central to self-esteem. Consider the following story told by a 40-year old American writer. He started writing plays in his twenties, when he lived in New York, and found almost instant success and fame. While still quite young, he married an entrancing young actress who had a part in one of his productions. Five years later, the couple moved to Los Angeles, leaving their friends and families in the East. Film scripts proved lucrative, and he bought a house on the ocean at Malibu, where they still live. Meanwhile, his wife's initially promising career began to fail. She started to drink heavily. His own career now began to falter. The critical acclaim he had once received turned to lack of interest, even contempt. He, however, had faith in his abilities and had recently invested a large amount of his own money in a film for which he had written the screenplay. It had failed badly. He had discovered in the last few weeks that, as a consequence of this failure, he would probably lose his Malibu home and be left with very little else. In addition to this disaster, his wife's drinking and their consequent rows had escalated over the last few months. One night she announced her decision to return to the East Coast in the hope of reviving her career. Divorce seemed inevitable.

The following morning he walked on the beach, his life in ruins. He was aware of a sense of strangeness and of feeling quite alone. He also began to realize that, despite all, he did not feel hopeless, despairing, or personally worthless. With everything stripped away, with apparently nothing left to live for, he experienced, as if within his chest, a kind of brightness and warmth, which he said was something like the sun. The sensation was nothing more than that, diffuse and without words or images. He knew then that he would not collapse and would be able to keep on going.

The writer's unusual experience seemed to be a concretization, or representation in bodily terms, of some core resource, some ultimate reservoir of optimism and well-being that could be called basic self-esteem. His story suggests that the heart of self-esteem is a feeling tone, which might perhaps be called *hedonic tone*.[2] This feeling-tone gives value to the experience in the way that value is attached to one's experiences of self (see Chapter 2). Jung (1935), perhaps, anticipated this idea when he wrote that "Feeling informs you through its feeling tones of the values of things" (p. 13).

The sense of value in self-esteem is curious because it cannot be defined in logical terms as a real thing. It is merely a feeling from which a sense of value is derived. One supposes that the gradual accumulation of such experiences leads to positive self-esteem in the way that Stanley Coopersmith (1967) defines it: "a *personal* judgement of worthiness" (p. 5). This definition seems to be the most suitable available.

Before looking for possible bases for the feeling-tone that gives value, we must consider the contributions of early writers to the understanding of self-esteem. Among the most significant was Harry Stack Sullivan. Sullivan's psychology depends upon three biological principles. The first is the principle of communal existence—"the living maintain constant exchange through their bordering membranes with certain elements in the physico-chemical universe around them" (Sullivan 1953, p. 31). In the human, this universe includes the social and cultural.

The organism may be in equilibrium or in relative disequilibrium with the environment. Sullivan conceived this equilibrium or otherwise in terms of the infant's needs, which at first are clearly physico-chemical. (It could be argued, although less clearly, that they are always physico-chemical.) These primary needs include obvious physico-chemical requirements such as oxygen and glucose, but also such needs as contact. The mother's absorbed observation of her child results in a perception of the infant's needs. This perception induces "a tension experienced as tenderness and as an impulsion to activities towards the relief of the infant's needs" (p. 39). Seen in this way, mother and baby are the two parts of a communal existence in which inbuilt signals in one trigger inbuilt responses in the other. Need is in a broad sense, disequilibrium in this dyadic system.

The next aspect of Sullivan's psychology is relevant to self-esteem. He introduces two polar constructs that relate to states of equilibrium or disequilibrium. They are absolute euphoria and absolute tension (terror). "Euphoria may be equated to a total equilibrium of the organism" (p. 37) and tension to disequilibrium. Sullivan was particularly concerned with the tension called anxiety. This "appertains to the infant's, and also to the mother's, communal existence with a *personal* environment" (p. 42). His emphasis was on the need to be rid of anxiety. He makes the important point, however, that the fulfillment of this need is not accompanied by euphoria. Rather, "the relaxation of the tension of anxiety, the re-equilibration of being in this specific respect, is the experience not of satisfaction, but of interpersonal *security*" (p. 42).

Sullivan's system mainly focuses on the origins of low self-esteem. The needs of the child, which are central to it, involve the tender emotions. The child has a need for tenderness and expresses this need through a display of emotions that in the adult are those of intimacy. A response such as mockery, contempt, or simple lack of interest devalues the intimate emotions, and the child is hurt in a way that feels like damage to the physical self. When the child lives in a situation where the exposure of the innermost feelings is dangerous, he learns to hide these emotions. He develops a pathology of privacy. Moreover, he learns that the social environment is made up of enemies. Although he lives among them, he is an isolate. There is no one who connects with that which is tender in him. He has undergone what Sullivan (1953) called "the malevolent transformation" (pp. 203–216). Where the disjunctions of this kind are great and repeated, a prevailing attitude of hatred will develop, and with it low self-esteem.

Sullivan's main thesis concerns the disaster of the social environment failing the growing child's need for tenderness. The contrary theme—the evolution of positive self-esteem—is not developed. Yet the seeds of it are there. Self-esteem must arise through an equilibrium with the social environment in which euphoria is generated. What might this equilibrium be?

The dance between the mother and baby, which is established by the age of 2 months, is the earliest example of this equilibrium. This engagement gives great pleasure to both mother and baby. Consider once again the following description from Mahler and colleagues (1975) "in which the 5–8 month old, surrounded by the admiring and libidinally mirroring, friendly adults, seemed electrified and stimulated by the mirroring admiration. This was evident by his excited wriggling of his body, bending his back to reach his feet or his legs, kicking and flailing with the extremities and stretching with an exaltedly pleasurable affect" (p. 221).

The baby shows he or she feels good. So do the adults. Their responses and body movements, in an escalation of emotion and bodily expression, fit in with each other. Mothers and other caregivers characteristically act in this way, naturally and without thinking about it. This is the kind of equilibrium from which come the moments of well-being that together make up a core of self-esteem. Kohut's ideas were similar. He even used the word *equilibrium*.

In his technical writing, Kohut (1971) would have seen the joyous wriggling of the excited infant as his exhibitionistic display and the pleased adult's responses as "mirroring the child's narcissistic-exhibitionistic enjoyment" (p. 116). This kind of language, to my mind, obscures the humanity of Kohut's intuition, which is found in his spoken words.

Like Sullivan, Kohut saw the baby triggering in the mother a particular response, which meshed with the baby's state. The response is a kind of irrational adoration, which he called "baby worship" (Elson 1987, p. 62). The baby's state is perhaps a delight in the self. "Whatever the baby does is responded to by the gleam in the mother's eyes, by her warmth, by her enthusiasm. Her self-esteem is heightened as she feels at one with the excited and exhibiting baby. It is this kind of an equilibrium, though on a much more silent level, that we are striving for all our lives" (p. 63).

Kohut makes clear that the interchange between mother and baby is truly reciprocal. Both partners' self-esteem is raised through their equilibrium, which I am calling *fit*.

A puzzle now arises. Why is the baby electrified? How does the sense of well-being arise? Nothing has been done to the baby. He has not been held or fed. There seems to be nothing actually going into him, as if it were a drug, which stimulates him. How can the mother's face induce a state of well-being? It is merely a collection of visual stimuli, which can have no obvious physical effects. We must now consider further the notion of fit. Henry Miller (1965) describes the following experience:

> It's as though I had no clothes on and every pore of my body was a window and all the windows open and the light flooding my gizzards. I can feel the light curving under the vault of my ribs and my ribs hang there over a hollow nave trembling with reverberations. How long this lasts I have no idea; I have lost all sense of time and place. After what seems like an eternity there follows an interval of semiconsciousness balanced by such a sheen, cool as jelly; and over this lake, rising in great swooping spirals, there emerge flocks of birds of passage with long slim legs and brilliant plumage. Flock after flock surge up from the cool, still surface of the lake and, passing under my clavicles, lose themselves in the white sea of space. And then slowly, very slowly, as if an old woman in a white cap were going the rounds of my body, slowly the windows are closed and my organs drop back into place. [p. 81]

This extraordinary account is of a response to music, that is, a mere collection of auditory stimuli. How could a sequence of noises provoke so profound an effect? Neurophysiology cannot be left out of an answer to this question.

In 1954, Olds and Milner discovered that electrical stimulation of certain parts of the brains of animals had a powerful effect. The animals would perform tasks to the point of exhaustion to gain such stimulation. This finding inspired considerable popular interest and the area that was the most strongly rewarding, the lateral hypothalamus, came to be called the pleasure center. Its function in humans and in our ordinary living can only be guessed at. It seems important, at least in my view, in the development of self-esteem. We now return to the experience of Henry Miller.

Music must trigger systems in the brain that are responsible for emotions. It follows from this assumption that there is, intrinsic to the central nervous system, the equivalent of a series of neuronal templates, which, as it were, recognize particular broad configurations of stimuli and, as a consequence of this recognition, emit a neurochemical response that determines mood, attention, and other mental states. Scherer and Oshinsky (1977) have made pioneering studies that support such an idea. Using a Moog synthesizer, they investigated the effect of different patterns of auditory stimuli in inducing emotions. By altering seven acoustic parameters, they were able to show that there was considerable agreement among judges for the mood-promoting effects of particular arrangements of tones. The moods included anger, surprise, sadness, and happiness.

It is evident that the mother, in her mirroring, is using her voice in a particular way that may have an effect like music. She is also visible. It seems likely that information about faces is genetically encoded.

Fantz was a pioneer in this area, and his studies have become very well known. His work suggested that the form of the human face was the most significant visual stimulus of all those confronting it. For example, he found (1963) that babies only 2 to 6 days old paid more attention to a disc with human features painted on it than to other stimuli of similar shape and size. Although other investigators have not been able to replicate some of his findings, and Fantz himself was forced to modify his original position (1965), there remains the strong possibility that the human being is prewired to respond to patterns of stimuli resembling faces. This is consistent with findings, which supported Darwin's original work of 1872, that certain repertoires of facial expression are part of our innate endowment.[3] Lewis (1969) was able to show that a preference for facelike patterns is shown at least during the first quarter year of life. The work of Spitz has made clear that the eyes are the most important feature of the face, at least until 2 months of age. The infant smiles at a mask of eyes but no mouth. Smiling in response to a face seems a central element of the kind of mother–baby interaction described by Mahler and her colleagues. How can this pattern of stimulus and response evoke pleasure? We must begin with the smile.

A blind baby, who obviously cannot imitate, will smile. At first, such a smile may seem random, but it is soon evident that the baby is smiling appropriately in response to such stimuli as the mother's voice (Schaffer, 1971). This apparently simple observation implies that the particular pattern of facial muscle contraction that makes up a smile is innate and somehow written into the brain. The pattern is triggered by only a narrow range of the multitude of stimuli enfolding the child at any moment. An important trigger for babies who are not blind is the smile of another.

It seems reasonable to assume a connection between the part of the brain that determines emotional states and the system in which is encoded the behavior of the smile, so that a neurophysiological link is made between a state of well-being, pleasure, or happiness and the behavior of a smile. This assumption gains some support from the work of Ekman (1983). He and his colleagues have conducted a series of fascinating studies on facial expression. In one of these, subjects were instructed in the laboratory to contract, one after the other, a number of facial muscles, so that the culmination was a recognizable emotional expression, such as hate or surprise. When the subjects were asked afterward what emotion they felt during the experiment, most of them named the emotion that was appropriate to the expression that had, as it were, been constructed for them, as if some kind of feedback effect were operating. While the actors made these facial muscle movements, their autonomic nervous system activity was recorded. Following this, they were asked to relive certain affect states, again while autonomic activity was recorded. Reproducing the facial muscle patterns evoked more clear-cut autonomic changes than reliving the emotion. Beebe and Lachmann (1988) comment on the interesting implications of this finding: "The implication is that by contracting the same facial muscles as perceived on another's face, the onlooker can literally feel the same autonomic sensations as the other person. Reproducing the expression of another (for example, in mirroring) can produce in the onlooker a similar state" (p. 15).

Ekman's (1983) findings are consistent with the idea that, at least for the behavior of smiling, there is a reverberation among a feeling of pleasure, the behavior of smiling, and the perception of another's smile. The baby smiles, the other smiles back; the baby feels pleased and smiles more broadly; the other smiles more broadly, vocalizing at the same time; the baby is now excited and wriggles and waves; at a certain peak of excitement either or both partners, (usually the baby) break the engagement for a while, allowing the excitement to wane; then the cycle may begin again. This, in broad terms, describes the cyclical behavior of mothers and infants, in which the behavior of each partner influences the behavior of the other, so that their pattern of activity is shared. There is a fit between the responses of the other and the experience of the baby.

So far, we have only touched upon self-esteem in infancy, yet it is clear that it goes on developing and changing throughout life. It is a dynamism, to use Sullivan's word. How does fit occur in the adult? We are concerned with something more complex than the reverberation between mother and child. The adult's smile, for example, is a far more complicated signal than that of an infant.

To follow the implications of Sullivan's thinking, self-esteem must involve the sense of what is intimate—the tender emotions. The experience of well-being arises with another. It comes when the match between response of the other and what one feels and knows is so good that brings with it a muted form of elation. There is a receptivity to, and a harmony with, the sensory environment, and things get "inside." This experience occurs in an intimate relationship and involves the totality of self including the body. Jean Rhys (1967) describes it:

> I am tuned up to top pitch. Everything is smooth, soft and tender. Making love. The colours of the pictures. The sunsets. Tender with colours when the sun sets—pink, mauve, green and blue. And the wind very fresh and cold and the lights in the canals like gold caterpillars and the seagulls swooping over the water. Tuned up to top pitch. Everything tender and melancholy—as life is sometimes, just for a moment. [p. 117]

From such descriptions we learn the parameters of well-being that make up self-esteem. There is a heightened sensation, a feeling of bodily smoothness, of flow, of the intensity of the moment.

The state of union described by Rhys is not necessarily associated with sexuality. Nevertheless, a sense of living a shared experience that is mutually understood brings with it an emotional state that necessarily involves the body. Bertrand Russell (1971) described a rare and unusually intense response to such an encounter. Of his first meeting with Joseph Conrad, he wrote:

We talked with continually increasing intimacy. We seemed to sink through layer after layer of what was superficial, till gradually both reached the central fire. It was an experience unlike any other that I have known. We looked into each other's eyes, half appalled and half intoxicated to find ourselves together in such a region. The emotion was as intense as passionate love, and at the same time all-embracing. I came away bewildered, and hardly able to find my way among ordinary affairs. [p. 209]

Russell's use of the word *intoxicated* implies a state involving chemistry and brings to mind the description of the electrified infant. How can mere words bring about such a state? This question is very like those asked about music and the human face. It seems that a resonance between inner and outer evokes a heightened sense of existence, a feeling tone. A mechanism that matches between sensory data and patterns encoded memorically or by other means must trigger this emotional state. Paul McLean (1969), who named the limbic system, suggested how it might come about.

McLean observed that the hippocampus and amygdala are essential to perception and are also connected to the hypothalamus and other parts of the brain involved in emotion. He suggested that all sensory input is funneled into the hippocampus and related areas. Their connection with the neurological systems underlying feeling states suggested at least "one possible mechanism by which the brain transforms the cold light which we see into the warm light with which we feel" (p. 271).

Here then is a hypothetical basis to the nature of fit and for a preliminary explanation of the profound effect of the precise and delicate ordering of auditory stimuli that we call music. It also gives us a way of understanding a feeling of self-esteem that is "something like the sun." It might evolve through the individual having lived enough of his or her life in a social environment that allows ordinary perception to be transformed into "the warm light with which we feel." McLean's words bring us back to the Californian scriptwriter who, as a last resource, felt something within him of brightness and warmth.

The fit we are talking of has involved the realm of the intimate and those experiences that are central to self. Yet this notion is very different from the vast literature on the subject, which focuses on goals, aspirations, and achievements. We come to the importance of a sense of agency. In considering the resonance between a psychic life broadly made up of thinking, feeling, and willing and the circumstances of the outside world, we have so far neglected the component of willing. Yet the awareness of one's willing being brought to fruition by one's action is one of the more fundamental matches between inner and outer that a child can experience. Charles Cooley (1902) was one of the first to comment on the significance of action, which, as it were, mirrors the wish. *Self-feeling*, to use his term

> appears to be associated chiefly with ideas of the exercise of power, of being a cause . . . the first definite thoughts that a child associates with self-feeling are probably those of his earliest endeavors to control visible objects—his limbs, his play things, his bottle and the like. Then he attempts to control the actions of the persons about him, and so his circle of power and self-feeling widens without interruption to the most complex of mature ambition. [pp. 145–146]

Jerome Kagan (1981), however, distinguishes between the child's apparent pleasure in simple motor activity and what he calls *mastery smiles*, which emerge during the second year of life. They reflect the child's pleasure in accomplishing planned tasks. The smile "follows prolonged investment of goal-directed effort— which serves a previously generated plan" (p. 57).

On the face of it, one can become one's own mirror simply by acting, by demonstrating, in a concrete way, a concordance between the wish and its fulfillment. This, indeed, is the basis of some therapeutic approaches to self-esteem. It is also the basis of the striving for high scores in the success/pretensions ratio used by some individuals as a means of overcoming a basic feeling of low self-esteem. It is a common observation that this is not generally achieved. In my view, the road to mastery begins with a basic feeling that arises when those emotions and ideas that are felt as peculiarly personal are responded to in a way that gives them value. George Brown and his colleagues (1986) found that in a relatively deprived South London suburb, self-esteem seemed to depend upon the amount of access to social supports and confiding relationships. The sense of mastery that arises through a sense of connectedness with another is the necessary precursor to action. Virginia Woolf (Nicholson 1975) described this feeling, akin to what Kohut might have called *grandiosity*. She wrote: "With regard to happiness—what an interesting topic that is! Walking about here with Jean for a companion, I feel a great mastery over the world" (p. 434).

The following clinical anecdote illustrates how responses from another, which match with one's personal and inner reality, are necessary before the environment can be acted upon in a way that further engenders self-esteem.

The patient's life was characterized by an almost total failure of mastery. She entered treatment with the specific complaint that she was unable to cope with the ordinary chores of day-to-day life. Her house remained in chaos despite her efforts to keep it tidy. She was not able to recommence her occupation as a draftswoman, although her two children were now at school. She remained at home in a state of helpless apathy.

Her parents had been incarcerated in a labor camp in the last part of World War II. She was born soon after in Europe. For about 5 years after the war, the family lived in various refugee camps and other temporary dwellings. It seemed clear that the patient's mother had been traumatized, was distracted, depressed, and presumably unable to give adequate attention to the child. After they arrived in Australia, both her parents worked, sometimes leaving the 5-year-old child alone in the house. The time of her life before Australia was never mentioned during her later development.

Despite these deprivations, the patient managed to train herself for a professional life. During her twenties she lived relatively uneventfully, working steadily. She married rather late, in her thirties, and had two children. Her husband was a commonsense kind of man, a carpenter. To the outside world, he would have seemed a perfectly reasonable companion and spouse. It appeared, however, that he consistently responded to her in a way that failed to recognize her own reality. This was illustrated by his behavior after their house had been flooded. This had occurred during a vacation and was caused by the husband's having made renovations that did not meet municipal standards. Since his carelessness would have disqualified their claims for insurance, he invented another story, which the insurance company accepted and which showed that the flood was caused by the patient's ineptitude. It was said that she had failed to turn off a tap before leaving for their holiday. The husband then retold this fiction to their friends and acquaintances as if it were fact. They joked with the patient about her stupidity. This event was emblematic of an existence in which her own inner states found no echo or resonating response in the outer world of others.

For about 15 years, she sought treatment, usually of a behavioral kind, for an inability to cope with her life and for a chronic low-grade depression. Nothing was successful. She entered the current treatment, conveying a desperate, yet resigned, helplessness. In a monotonous, somewhat querulous voice, she cataloged her endless failures, her hopelessness, and her boredom. The main therapeutic approach depended upon attempts to put into words, in a speculative way, what seemed to be her immediate personal reality. The therapist learned to eschew all interpretive behavior. The patient was able to explain that her inner states involved feelings that determined her behavior and that, on this basis, seemed perfectly comprehensible. Responses that attempted to give meaning to her states in a cognitive way made her experience seem unreasonable and even stupid. She would relapse into her zone of apathy, depression, and helplessness. The therapist's second main contribution to the therapeutic conversation was to give appropriate responses to spontaneous emotional expression.

After about 6 months, she seemed remarkably different. There were times when her demeanor had vitality and energy. During sessions her spontaneous laughter conveyed a sense of pleasure. Moreover, she spoke of days during which she experienced joy.

The particular session that is relevant to this discussion occurred the day before the patient had to confront a difficult task. She tried to describe how coming to therapy was going to help her meet her responsibility and to overcome the dead weights that seemed to drag her down. The description was difficult because it involved something intangible. She spoke of the need "to touch base again." This experience had the effect of, as she said, "lifting me out." This state of being lifted contrasted with her more usual experience of being "a lone planet by myself." She said: "I'm given permission to exist here. That person says you're okay. You can join the human club. If I don't have that connection, I'm spinning off on my own in space."

The therapist picked up the phrase about the human club. The patient laughed, as if enjoying the conversation. "Yes, I've got a membership ticket." Following this, she said: "I feel sort of a loss, of my, you know, my self-esteem, that I get so churned up over it [i.e., tomorrow's task]. It's quite funny when you think about it (laughs, then sighs). You know, a person of value doesn't . . . someone with dignity or integrity doesn't do that to themselves, get churned up over such a little thing. It's sort of demeaning. I feel I demean myself to make such a big thing about it."

In essence, the patient describes a general sense of disconnectedness, of being "a lone planet." With the therapist, she achieves a sense of connection, of touching base, out of which arises a feeling of being lifted, which involves energy and positive feeling. This will enable her to have sufficient mastery to act capably the following day. She realizes that for someone with good self-esteem, a feeling of mastery and being able to cope is not a problem. In contrast, from the negative point of view, she sees that lack of mastery has a feedback effect, diminishing a sense of personal value. It is of interest that the therapist has not used the words *value* and *self-esteem* and has little theoretical interest in the subject.

In summary, basic self-esteem consists of an almost inexpressible feeling that arises in relation to others whose responses fit. This feeling involves warmth and value. The hedonic tone produced by fit presumably has a neurophysiological basis, which, as yet, can only be speculated upon. Although self-esteem is not an idea, ideas arise from it. One of these ideas is mastery and from it comes plans for action and their ultimate fulfillment. The match between the plan and its enactment in the external world provides another kind of fit. The evolution of self-esteem throughout life is a dynamism, involving reverberations between a core sense of self-esteem and the responses of others to expressions and actions that one feels as peculiarly personal. Those that match the central experience of inner life add to a feeling of personal worth.

Part II | **DISRUPTION**

Chapter 9 | BODY FEELING AND DISJUNCTION

The experience of connectedness, or fit, in being with another involves subtle bodily feelings, such as an enhanced feeling of the body's rhythms, of its smoothness, flow, and spatiality. In this chapter, we approach the contrary state, in which connectedness with the other is lost and the sense of self diminished. We return to the notion of the two playrooms.

The playing child feels good. Alerting stimuli break up this state, however briefly. Something happens that is not part of or related to the child's thought processes and feeling and that causes him or her to become conscious of something else. Mundane events cause the child to direct his or her attention away from playing and toward this event. The change is accompanied by subtle alterations in affect and bodily function. The child's face may show interest, and there is a desynchronization of the electroencephalograph, a fall in skin resistance, and often a slight drop in heart rate.[1] Thus changes go on in the body while at the same time there is a shift in emotional tone.

The intermittent interruption of the patterns of play does not always come through actual stimuli. Sometimes the alerting is

77

due to the kind of response made by the other, who, as selfobject, provides the enabling atmosphere of play. As the child plays, he or she is continuously making and remaking a personal reality. When the parents show the child that they are not part of this reality, that their experience is somehow outside that of the child rather than within it, alerting occurs and play stops. The parents' inaccurate, insufficient, or, in other ways, inadequate attunement to the child's reality might seem minor to an observer or may not even be perceived. In essence, however, it does not fit in. It seems *estranged* from the immediate reality of the child. This awareness of the *strangeness* of an element of the perceived environment is part of the fundamental means of our coping. It needs to be discussed in further detail.

We live in an environment that is largely predictable, expectable, and familiar. Much of our behavior in dealing with this environment is automatic. We pick up cups, turn door handles, walk up stairs, taking little notice of what we do. If, however, the cup seems unusually heavy, the door handle turns too far, or our footfall on one of the stairs sounds different from the rest, our attention is aroused. These things are strange. A neurological mechanism is constantly operating during waking life matching perceptions against memories, including very recent memories, of past experience. This matching leads to a judgment of familiar or strange.[2] What is familiar may be screened out, so that it does not reach consciousness. The capacity to screen out what is familiar and not relevant is necessary to our ordinary coping.[3] We could not manage our lives if every one of the myriad actions of potential sensation surrounding us impinged upon consciousness. We could not read a newspaper in a train or listen to a conversation at a party if all the potentially audible sounds were heard. We suppose, in ordinary development, that the parent is often experienced as part of the familiar environment, by responding in a way that is consistent with the child's continuing reality. The parent, however, is far from irrelevant. His or her familiarity is not screened out. Rather, the parent's activity is not salient. The child does not particularly attend to the parent in the same way that she does not notice the movements of her hands as she dresses a doll or picks a flower. If, however, something went wrong with this movement, the child would immediately notice it. In the same way, the mother not responding and staying stock still would seem strange, even frightening. The selfobject is both active and nonsalient.

Those with disorders of self have frequently experienced a chaotic family life in which alerting stimuli repeatedly impinge upon them, preventing the development of self. An equivalent disruption, however, can occur when there is no overt disturbance in the family. Severe disjunctions between the child's immediate personal reality and the response of a caregiver will impact upon the child like a loud noise. Chronic alerting can be a consequence of ongoing failures in parental empathy. Where the parental environment is repeatedly and habitually unattuned, the child is constantly alerted, breaking up the field of play. The child is now consistently oriented outward with little chance to develop a sense of self. There is nothing much inside, no *real me*. There is also, for some people, a persisting feeling of estrangement.

Those affected with disorders of self are peculiarly sensitive to the other's failures of attunement. Indeed, a vulnerability to the sense of disjunction between one's own reality and the response of the other is a central feature of the borderline syndrome. The effect of such a disjunction varies in intensity. We now consider in more detail the nature of a disjunction.

At this point, it is necessary to emphasize that disjunctions are necessary to normal development. We have seen that, in a metaphorical sense, the child of, say, 2 or 3 years, inhabits two playrooms, one real and the other partly illusory. He or she oscillates between two states of being with the other. Where one or the other of these experiences is deficient or lacking, development is impeded. Just as the child needs the parent who is attuned to his or her personal reality, the child also needs experiences when the other is not felt as part of this reality. These experiences help to establish the concept of self boundary, since they bring into the child's awareness an outside world that contrasts with the world that is inner. A hypothetical parent who was always perfectly attuned to the child would create a psychotic. Disjunctions in this sense have a positive value.[4] It is clear, however, that it is much easier to trigger the state associated with alerting than the state that depends upon a selfobject experience. The latter condition is fragile, easily lost early in development and in those with disorders of self. These people have little access to a zone that is potentially inner. Their existence involves a hypertrophy of the real.

We may divide disjunctions into those of a positive kind and those that have a negative affect. Let us start with the former, using ordinary experience.

Someone says, "Have you seen L'Atalante?" You are interested, curious. You reply, "What is L'Atalante?" Attention is outer-directed, toward the questioner as object. The language is linear, logical, and goal-directed. At the same time, however, there is no loss of inner experience. It is merely put on hold.

The negative disjunction also precipitates an experience of the other as salient, a form of attention that is outer directed, and language that is linear. Its effect, however, is different in two important ways. First, there is a diminishment of the sense of interior life. Second, the affect is negative. There are, I believe, three main categories of affective change perhaps intermingling, which are triggered in somewhat different ways. They are loss of vitality, anger (and sometimes sadness), and anxiety. Each has its own mechanism. We consider them in turn.

The first category of response can be understood in terms of the self-esteem system described in the previous chapter. Where a disjunction occurs, the experiences are the opposite of those produced by a feeling of oneness with another. There are changes in the sense of vitality, of the unity of being, and of personal spatiality.

Connectedness with the other is associated with enlivenment, as in the example of the baby who was electrified. A disjunction is followed by a sense of deadness, a loss of vitality, conveyed perhaps in the tone of voice, even in the body, which might sag as if in dejection. Furthermore, when we feel in harmony with another, there is a sense of unity of being and of flow. Both these experiences are lost with disjunction. There is a breaking up of experience. The conversation may have a desultory, fragmented quality that may approach incoherence. There is a sense of loss of bodily rhythm, of stasis, and of nothing happening, the opposite of flow.

In addition to these changes, there may be an alteration in the experience of personal space. When we feel at one with someone else, there is a sense of personal expansion. This too is lost with disjunction. Instead, the feeling is of constriction. In extreme cases, one's experience of self no longer corresponds with the dimensions of the actual body. The individual may feel shrunken or sticklike. One woman, who was both sensitive and verbally adept, described this curious state in a number of ways: "I feel the essence of me has shrunk. My body feels tiny. When I look out my arms seem grotesquely large but only because I'm diminished. I know my body is really the normal size, but. . . ." These states of personal constriction were accompanied by boredom, deadness, and dissatisfaction. She eventually discovered that they seemed to be related to her feeling cut off from her husband, her children, and her therapist.

The second category of response to a disjunction arises where it is felt, in extreme cases, like an attack upon "the secret." It has an effect analogous to a physical blow. The behavior of the other, which seems to damage the integrity and value of those feelings and ideas that are precariously held as a core of self, is felt as an assault. There is an immediate flare of anger, a lashing out, which is sometimes called narcissistic rage. Alternatively, instead of lashing out, the individual may slump as if actually hit.

This response can again be understood in terms of the ideas expressed in the second chapter. When we expose those experiences, fantasies, ideas, memories, and feelings that are peculiarly personal and intimate, highly valued, and sensed as part of our core, there is a chance that the responses of others may invalidate, damage, or devalue this central aspect of self. Exposure risks the experience of shame. In extreme circumstances, shame is devastation, associated with loss of a sense of personal worth.

Such responses occur in the therapeutic situation and are generally inadvertent. For example, a therapist attempting to enter into the experience the patient was describing said, "You must have felt ashamed." The patient became enraged, interpreting this response as meaning that her behavior was shameful. Quite small slights may trigger unexpected rage in those with disorders of self.

The third category of affective response to disjunction, which ranges through anxiety and emptiness to annihilation, can be understood through its effect upon the sense of existence. In ordinary circumstances, our customary feeling of going-on-being cannot be removed. In childhood, however, it is precarious. This idea was anticipated by Descartes. Where William James had concluded that our sense of existence depended upon the flow of inner life, Descartes (1637–1641) went beyond him. He conceived a possible end to this sense of existence. He wrote: "*I am, I exist:* this is certain; but for how long? For as long as I think, for it might be, if I ceased to think, that I would at the same time cease to exist" (p. 105). His remarks suggest a threat. Yet the removal of thoughts in adult life is unimaginable except in some kinds of psychotic terror. In infancy, however, it is possible. How thoughts may be removed can be understood, once again, by considering the child's play.

As the child plays, his thoughts are in the things with which he plays. Their removal means, at the same time, a removal of the thoughts connected with them. In this sense, thought is substantial. It is now possible to understand to some extent the apprehensions of the shy young woman described in Chapter 1. She too conceived thoughts as substantial so that to express them carried with it the feeling that she was losing parts of her physical self. Her experience may have been like that of the 2-year-old who screams when his toys are taken away. Emptiness is the result. Going-on-being can be threatened in a second way, through the absence of the other who provides the atmosphere in which it can occur. The child or the person whose sense of self is frail is now in the situation imagined by Descartes. Existence is under threat. A fear of something like annihilation arises. For the individual whose development of self has been disrupted, quite small breaks with the other who is experienced as selfobject bring a tremor, a sense of unease, a fear that is like teetering on the edge of a void.

In the clinical situation, the most important disjunctions are inadvertent. Their detection and explanation offer significant opportunities for therapeutic change, as will be seen later in Chapter 17. However, disjunctions may also result from the therapist's training and theoretical background. An obvious example, no longer common, is of the therapist who adopts the blank screen stance of classical psychoanalysis. Another, more common, involves therapeutic responses that are designed to show the meaning of the patient's remarks, behavior, feelings, and fantasies. These are often helpful where they show an understanding of the patient's experience. Where they are disjunctive and rejected by the patient, the therapist may conceive this response in terms of resistance. Repetition of the therapist's view of the patient's reality, and the meaning of his or her experience, may lead to an undermining of a fragile sense of existence. The therapist may have inflicted upon the patient a state of estrangement and depersonalization (Meares and Hobson 1977).

Disjunctions, however, usually come about in more subtle ways, such as tone of voice, gaze, and the way in which words are used. A particular kind of grammar, for example, an excessive use of pronouns or of questions, sets up a situation to which the therapist places him- or herself in the role of object rather than selfobject.

Finally, however, and this is most important, therapy usually begins in a state of disjunction. Those with disorders of self usually live in a state of chronic disjunction. Since the person must be seen as part of a larger organism that includes others, the therapist begins to feel something of the bodily unease, the disconnectedness, of the patient. The therapist may not quite be aware of this disconnectedness since the conversation may seem unremarkable, concerning subjects that seem relevant and important. Nevertheless, the therapist may begin to respond on the basis of the disjunction to him or her that has been brought about by the patient. The therapist begins to ask questions, to use technical words, to make intellectual contributions to the encounter. The sense of disjunction is compounded. Both partners are caught in a reverberating situation that might be called *intersubjective*,[5] in which the behavior of each cannot be understood alone but includes their effect upon each other. This entrapment is further explored in Chapter 11. The danger of this situation, if unrecognized, is that it has consequences that may be acted out beyond the boundaries of the therapeutic situation. The patient, now affected with a painful emptiness, takes steps to alleviate it. This may take a symbolic and apparently self-destructive form. The following is an example of such an attempt.

> Mr. P. was a 35-year-old businessman who presented with a vague depression that was akin to a chronic sense of dissatisfaction with life. He was afflicted by a sense of deadness and emptiness and had low self-esteem.
>
> Mr. P. was tall and strongly built. His voice was at times menacing; at others, petulant. His demeanor was tense. His story

soon revealed disturbances consistent with the diagnosis of borderline personality. It also showed a person of considerable courage and persistence in that he had overcome the adversity of a very disadvantaged childhood and had become an engineer in a senior position in a construction company. He was in charge of large projects and was seen as competent and a hard man. Other aspects of his life were less functional. His second marriage of 2 years was failing, partly as a consequence of his compulsive promiscuity.

During sessions, he characteristically stared into space, delivering a monologue that frequently had a paranoid flavor and conveyed the idea that he had been unjustly served by life. If I made any significant intervention, the response was often similar to that of a startle reaction. He would say "What!" and look around as if surprised to discover there was another person in the room.

On this particular occasion, the session began in the usual way. After about 10 minutes, however, Mr. P. began to work himself into a rage. He announced that following the session he would follow a woman, any woman he saw in the street. A few minutes later he enlarged upon this, threatening to follow her to her home. Finally, he demanded to know what I was going to do when he had raped the woman, when the case reached the courts and the newspapers, and when my name was mentioned. Indeed, he demanded, in a threatening manner, to know what I was going to do to stop him.

Listening to this monologue of escalating vehemence, even violence, I became aware that it had been broken up by tiny pauses. On reflection, I also realized that, without being quite aware of it, I usually filled those miniature silences with some brief, nonverbal vocalization, such as a grunt or a murmur. I realized that on this occasion, I had not responded in this way. I then said that something had been going very wrong during the previous few minutes and speculated that it might have been related to my behavior during the pauses, that Mr. P. might have felt that I was not listening.

Mr. P. responded by saying I was like his mother, who never listened. He went on to describe her behavior, his violence diminishing as he did so. She was constantly belittling him, comparing him adversely with his elder sister, the perfect child. In an attempt to be heard, he, as it were, turned up the volume, becoming a brash and noisy child. She retaliated by beating him fiercely or, at the least, attacking him verbally. He could remember her only as cold, brittle, rejecting, and as having so emasculated his father that he spent a great deal of time away from the house. Mr. P. imagined that the family's emigration from the north of England to Australia during his adolescence was their attempt to hold their marriage together.

The conversation progressed to where the patient was able to describe the fantasy associated with the as yet unknown woman in the street. He imagined standing in the garden outside the window as the woman undressed. His greatest wish was not particularly erotic in the ordinary sense. He wanted her to look up, see him, and gaze upon him with admiration. The woman's gaze of admiration was to provide a mirroring, which compensated for the failure of mirroring during the silences. It seemed reasonable to infer that his perverse sexual activity was supposed to reconstitute, however briefly or maladaptively, a disintegrating sense of self.

Chapter 10 | REVERSALS

The individual's state of going-on-being is disrupted by a sense of disconnection or disjunction between him or her and the other as selfobject. Disjunction is shown by changes in affect, for example, deadness, tension, anger; by linear thinking; by external orientation, for example, toward events rather than feelings or memories; and in extreme circumstances, to the mere stimuli of the present. In this chapter the description is extended to include changes in who-one-is. I focus on a particular aspect of this experience, the instability of which is characteristic of those with disorders of self. It involves certain pathologies of identification, which I call *reversals*.

The changes in who-one-is in those with disorders of self might be figuratively conceived as occurring, at any moment, in three dimensions. First, there is a range of selves, occurring in the present, who are good, bad, likeable, incompetent, and so on, who, as it were, are confronting and linking to a range of experiences of the other. Self-state, here, occurs along a horizontal plane. A second category of experiences is vertical, fluctuating along a chronological axis. The individual's states range between those of a young person and those of someone who is more nearly mature. The third dimension is also in the horizontal plane, orthogonal to the first. It involves a back-and-forth change in which the subject *becomes* the other. This chapter concerns this last axis in which there is an oscillation between the poles of self and the other. The change is often sudden, salient, and perplexing. I begin with two examples.

REVERSALS AND THE INTEGRITY OF SELF

The first case is of a woman of 19. She has a history of multiple suicide attempts. She is talking with a trainee psychiatrist who has recently become her therapist and is asking him about the suitability of multiple sexual liaisons. The question has arisen because several men have told her they wished to live with her. Within a few sentences of listening to her, however, the therapist finds himself accused of advocating a life of sexual license. The patient reprimands him for this moral stance. The therapist is bewildered because, as far as he knows, he has done nothing of the kind. What is particularly baffling for him is that there has been a very rapid shift in roles. At one moment the girl is treating him like a parent, asking for advice about the complexities of relationships of late adolescent life. A few moments later *she* becomes the parent, lecturing him about morality.

A second and more subtle reversal comes from a patient who does not have a borderline personality, although she could be described as having a disorder of self. She is sophisticated and intelligent and is telling the therapist about a book she has been reading. The therapist's response is misinterpreted by the patient and sensed as belittling. A few sentences later, without apparent reason, the therapist finds that she is being lectured to by the patient, whose subject is Freudian theory, of which the patient has a very comprehensive grasp. Once again the therapist is perplexed by a reversal of roles, which, in this case, finds the patient switching from something like a child–pupil role to that of parent–teacher.

What has happened in these two cases? Before attempting an answer, I give two more illustrations of reversals. The first is a well-known case reported by Karl Abraham (1924). A woman was very attached to her father. In Abraham's words, she clung to him "with all an unmarried daughter's love" (p. 434). A terrible crisis occurred in her life when he was discovered to be a thief and was arrested. As a consequence, she became psychotically depressed. The main feature of this psychosis was that she held the delusional belief that *she* was a thief. It was as if having lost her father, not only in a physical sense since he was now in prison, but also her idealized idea of him, she now *became* him.

The second story also concerns loss. Simone de Beauvoir (1969) described her experience after visiting her mother in the hospital following an operation during which it was discovered that her mother was in the last stages of cancer. Her response was catastrophic. She went home late at night, and after an outburst of tears, talked to Sartre:

> I talked to Sartre about my mother's mouth as I had seen it that morning and about everything I had interpreted in it—greediness refused, an almost servile humility, hope, distress, loneliness—the loneliness of her death and of her life—that did not want to admit its existence. And he told me that my own mouth was not obeying me any more: I had put Maman's mouth on my own face and in spite of myself, I copied its movements. Her whole person, her whole being, was concentrated there, and compassion wrung my heart. [p. 28]

In a much smaller way, only detected by someone who knew her well, de Beauvoir also showed a reversal following catastrophic loss.

Might it be that the transient reversals shown in the first two examples had a somewhat similar basis? That is, they were responses to miniature losses that precipitated a disruption of the sense of self. This, then, is the hypothesis: *reversals are a consequence of a severe disruption of the sense of self.* This disruption occurs when there is a disjunction or disconnection with the other who is sensed as necessary to the subject's going-on-being, that is, the selfobject. Where the other is not available as selfobject, or physically not there, then the threat to self emerges. The reversal is an attempt to shore up a sense of existence by becoming the necessary other who has gone.

How does this idea help us to understand the first two vignettes? In the first case the girl was frightened by the possibilities that confronted her. Although she seemed confident, in fact she was scared, not knowing how to cope with the men around her. The therapist, however, responded to her in a manner that he considered to be nonjudgmental. There was nothing particularly wrong with this response except that he did not pick up her anxiety, and so, for her, there was a feeling of being grossly misunderstood. A disconnection or disjunction occurred of which the therapist was unaware. In the second case, the therapist did not realize that the book about which the patient spoke had an intense personal significance for the patient. Although the therapist tried to respond in a way that was empathic, the response was not perceived in this way. Once again the patient was not understood, and a disconnection or disjunction occurred of a very subtle kind. In both these cases, then, we postulate that the reversal is a consequence of a break in the sense of connectedness between self and selfobject such that it was experienced as a threat to that individual's sense of existence, although this threat was slight and transient compared with the massive losses of Abraham's patient and of Simone de Beauvoir. A reversal, then, is the consequence of a pathological situation in which anxiety of a fundamental kind is aroused, in which something akin to annihilation or disintegration is momentarily experienced.

It was perhaps Anna Freud who first drew attention to the phenomenon that I call reversals. In her essay "Identification with the Aggressor" (1966), she suggested that behavior that seemed to mimic the other was a form of defense against an anxiety that had been precipitated not long before. At the beginning of the essay, she gives an example of a boy who made faces in class. These were so gross that at times the whole class would burst out laughing. When the child was examined in conjunction with the teacher, the psychologist Aichorn saw that "the boy's grimaces were simply a caricature of the angry expression of the teacher and that, when he had to face a scolding by the latter, he tried to mask his anxiety by involuntarily imitating him. The boy identified himself with the teacher's anger and copied his expression as he spoke, though the imitation was not recognized. Through his grimaces he was assimilating himself to, or identifying himself with the dreaded external object" (A. Freud, p. 113). As A. Freud put it: "A child introjects some characteristic of an anxiety object and so assimilates an anxiety experience which he has just undergone" (p. 113). How do these ideas of defense relate to the phenomenon I am describing?

If we consider the first example of the girl besieged by several men, we find that a reversal is indeed due to anxiety. There are, however, two levels to the anxiety. The first is the anxiety about not knowing how to manage her relationships. Underneath this is a second and more fundamental anxiety, which arises from *the failure of the therapist* to understand her feelings. This anxiety, which arises through the disjunction and which poses momentarily and in a limited way a threat to the sense of existence, is fundamental. This latter and more primitive kind of anxiety seems to be the necessary trigger to a reversal. Following this postulate, one would suppose that the boy who made faces was not merely afraid of scolding. Underlying this fear, presumably, was a more basic and powerful form of terror associated with a disintegration of self.

We next consider whether, in fact, a reversal is a defense. I am saying that a reversal is a consequence of a situation in which there is a loss of connection with the other, who is felt as necessary to going-on-being. When the other fails as a selfobject, the child, or the patient, responds by taking on for him- or herself a salient aspect of the other in order to shore up a threatened sense of existence. In that the reversal is a response to anxiety, it is a defense. It is not, however, the kind of defense proposed by A. Freud. She conceived the child's angry appearance as a defense against an "external object" (p. 110). It was meant to frighten the aggressor. However, I would speculate that the basis of this boy's behavior was different. Most children are afraid of a scolding, but they do not make bizarre faces. It seems not unreasonable to suppose that when the reversal occurred, the little boy was so afraid of the teacher that all sense of self had been obliterated. The story of this boy suggests the possibility that originally in the child's development, *the behavior of the other at the point of the disjunction becomes the behavior of the subject during the reversal.*

REVERSAL AND TRANSFERENCE

Further evidence concerning reversals following disruptions of the self–selfobject bond comes from a study whose principal aim was to evaluate the outcome of those with severe personality disorders treated according to the principles of a psychology of self, using trainee therapists working under close supervision. As far as can be judged, the report of the findings describes the first prospective follow-up, at least in the English language literature, of outpatient psychotherapy of any kind with borderline patients (Stevenson and Meares 1992). All sessions were audiotaped with the patients' written consent. These tapes showed that disjunctions of the self–selfobject connectedness produced not only affect shifts, but also changes in language toward that which was more linear and outer directed. They also precipitated transference phenomena, which, when the disjunction was severe, sometimes involved the mechanism of reversal. Following is an example:

> The patient is 35. Her background includes repeated sexual abuse by her father with which, apparently, her mother colluded. The mother was an unstable woman who was neglectful of her daughter and whose responses to her were unpredictable. The patient has been admitted to a psychiatric hospital more than thirty times with manifestations of borderline personality, including quasipsychotic phenomena, suicide attempts, and self-mutilation. She has responded to a change in session time by mutilating herself. At the beginning of the following session, the therapist notices that there is something different about the patient and remarks upon it. There is no initial response, but after about 10 minutes she says: "The only thing I can sort of think when I arrived, I had been pondering on what was different about it . . . the only thing I can think of (pause) y' know, I felt such utter contempt towards you."
>
> She then went on to talk about anger and how she wanted to hurt her husband when he hurt her. This, however, was an ordinary anger, different from the extraordinary anger she had felt for her therapist and which, although this was not made explicit, was expressed during her self-mutilation. The therapist replied by saying: "I was wondering if it seemed I was contemptuous of you, that I was sort of dismissing you and your feelings." The patient replied: "Yeah, well it sort of felt like I'd been given the bum's rush." The therapist said: "I wondered if you'd had that feeling with your mum, that she was contemptuous of you." The patient replied: "Very much, mm. Irrespective of what I thought or felt or what I would have liked to have been, if she'd already decided on something, it didn't matter, I didn't enter into the conversation."
>
> Later in the session, the patient described the background of her self-mutilation. When she was 6 or 7, she found that the only time

she would get a hug from her mother was when she hurt herself accidentally. She then started to cut herself to gain this solace. It soon began to fail as her mother realized what was happening and reverted to her system of neglect. Nevertheless, the child found that cutting herself was still soothing. There remained within the act of cutting something of the soothing effect of her mother's care. The patient described it: "I remember I used to feel much better inside. I didn't feel so empty, so lonely somehow." In this way, the self-mutilation, which involved something of a reversal, was an integrating act.

A relationship between reversals and transference phenomena is evident in the reverberations of contempt. We might suppose that originally, the child's integrity of self was threatened by parental contempt. In the current situation, the disjunction between self and selfobject comes about in another way. Nevertheless, there is a reversal during which the patient becomes contemptuous. Furthermore, she perceives the therapist as also contemptuous. Put another way, the reversal is accompanied by a transference experience (see Chapter 17).

A second illustration of a relationship between reversal and transference comes from the therapy of another borderline patient who also suffered severe anorexia nervosa. Her relationship with her mother was fused, or symbiotic. In other words, there was little sense of boundary between the child's subjective space and that of the mother. Accordingly, the mother was able to inflict severe sanctions upon the child by withdrawal. When this occurred, the patient was threatened with a sense of annihilation. The session—which has been preceded by a severe disjunction, the therapist's vacation—opens with the patient withdrawn and practically mute. Later in the session the patient is able to say that she experiences the therapist as withdrawn and cut off, although the tape shows this to be very far from the case.

In this case, also, a severe disjunction brings about a reversal in which the patient replicates the role of the original other in the earlier trauma. However, she also experiences the other of the present in the same way.

INTROJECTS

How do these ideas relate to previous conceptualizations? In particular, is a reversal an introjection, the word A. Freud had used? Since introjection is frequently seen to be a product of anxiety, notably in Kleinian theory, it resembles a reversal. One of the problems, however, about the word *introjection* is that it is used to describe not only a pathological situation based on anxiety, but also a normal one. For example, Melanie Klein, in her famous 1955 paper "On Identification," wrote that "identification as a sequel to introjection is part of normal development" (p. 141).[1] This collapsing of pathology and normality into one concept seems unsuitable. There is a case for retaining the use of the term *introjection*, or *introject*, but using it in a specific and confined way.

I suggest that an introject is the end product of a reversal that has become relatively fixed. Since it is hedged about with anxiety, it cannot be integrated within the self representation. The introject is "undigested" (Kohut 1971, p. 49). As Glasser (1986) suggests, introjection might be seen as an incomplete process. The object does not become part of the self but remains within, separate, sometimes experienced as an alien.

The normal process of identification is different. It is anxiety-free and is fostered by an atmosphere in which the individual feels understood. Its first phase is simple copying. For example, a little boy of 2 swaggers around with his hands in his pockets, looking like his father. This is different from the first stage of introjection, the reversal, which is almost echopraxic at times, for example, the case of the little boy who made faces. There is little distinction between self and other. In contrast, the 2-year-old who is swaggering around like his father shows this distinction. He is *not* his father. He is *like* him. It is *as if* he were his father. His behavior has about it a duality described by Stern (1985), who writes: "To perform delayed imitations, infants must have two versions of the same reality available: the representation of the original act, as performed by the model, and their own actual execution of the act. Furthermore, they must be able to go back and forth between these two versions of reality and make adjustments of one or the other to accomplish a good imitation" (p. 164).

Identification progresses, we suppose, from a first stage in which the experience of the other is taken in as an aliment, a kind of perceptual food. Gradually, through the processes of assimilation and accommodation, the object representation is taken into the self representation completely. Sandler and Rosenblatt (1962) use the metaphor of shape for this process. At the completion of the taking in of the object representation, the self representation, as it were, changes shape. The form of the original other can no longer be found. This is the opposite of the reversal in which the lack of integration causes self to be experienced not as a single shape but as a conglomerate. The absence of duality, or poor differentiation between self and object, together with the imped-iment to integration imposed by anxiety, leads to a collapsing together, into each other, of experiences of self and experiences of the other, without space between them. This is exemplified by the patient who was contemptuous. When she cut herself before the session, at least three experiences could be distinguished. First, there was the child hurting herself, second, there was the child hurting someone else, and third, there was the mother soothing the child: three people, as it were, on top of each other.

In some cases, the undigested nature of the introject is extreme. The individual has the experience of being occupied or inhabited by somebody else. Following is an example:

> A woman, frightened about her anger toward her small son, enters therapy. There is a background of physical abuse by her father. During one session she is able to describe her strange experience when she was about to strike her son. She said: "I saw my dad and me in place of me and John (her son). Him yelling and screaming and threatening me. Getting ready to hit me. Fear, like a knot, in that situation. I was feeling it as a little girl. It was the same feeling I'd had through my whole life, which is the trigger for a worrying situation." She went on to say: "I didn't want to be like that. The awful thing, I was repeating a memory that was totally abhorrent to me and I didn't want to be like. I had no control. I always said I would never be like him and here it was happening beyond my control. It was as if it were subconscious, like I was being controlled by something out of my power. It was like being demonized. Like having someone in your body making you speak and making you act, even though you're fighting it the whole time. Like your body's not your own. You don't have control of your body or your speech."

This description supports the notion that a reversal first occurs in a situation of high anxiety, even terror. Accounts such as these are helpful in trying to understand the phenomenon of the victim of abuse later becoming a perpetrator. Such behavior is not explicable in terms of, say, learning theory. The theoretical position put forward here leads to the prediction that the reversal is produced by the more extreme form of abuse, in which little remains of the sense of self. This idea conforms with the observations of some authorities in this area. Steele (1986), for example, notes that:

> Although there is no absolute correlation between the type of maltreatment occurring in infancy and the type of maltreatment expressed in later life by the adult parent, there seems to be a tendency toward direct literal repetition. Victims of more severe physical punishment tend to repeat the severe spankings and whippings with belts which they have undergone. [p. 285]

Literal repetition, rather than a digested or transmuted form of internalization, is a principal characteristic of the phenomenon of reversal.

We might suppose that in some individuals, the reversal is relatively enduring, more nearly conforming to the usual concept of an introject. The possibility is illustrated by the following history.

> The patient was a woman of 30. She had survived a childhood characterized by terrifying physical abuse from her father. Her way of trying to maintain something of herself during these beatings was, as she afterwards wrote, to "retreat within myself where they could not get me." She would never cry: "There was only me to comfort myself and to try and stay strong." Afterwards she would remain alone in her bedroom. "I would sit up in bed and then I would get very angry as well and I would hit my head on the metal bedhead. I liked this and started to relieve my feelings this way. I was in my early teens when I started cutting myself."
>
> Despite these traumata, she managed to function socially. She was able to work and she married in her twenties. She had two children. Not surprisingly, she had fears of harming them and had, in fact, done so. She entered therapy after a series of serious suicide attempts. Her history of self-mutilation and shoplifting then emerged. Both activities were associated with a "high." Her marriage was distant and asexual.
>
> Although quite a small woman, she gave the impression of being a man masquerading as a female. Her clothing was non-

descript. She usually wore jeans. She dangled a handbag as if it were a totally unfamiliar object. It soon became evident that she identified with male violence. She trained with heavy weights and learned martial arts. At nights she sometimes wandered in parks in the hope of being accosted by a man so that she could retaliate by beating him up.

Therapy was extremely difficult. Her tension would sometimes rise alarmingly during sessions so that on occasion she would leap from her chair and smash her head on the wall or windowsill, once requiring suturing. She was frequently silent. However, she was able to explain in writing something of her experience. It seemed that there was an "otherside" inside her, which she called an "it" and which felt alien to her. At times, it took control. She wrote: "I feel the otherside always preoccupying my thoughts when I'm in therapy. I lose control of how I want the session to go. It seems it is deliberately ruining it for me, as if I don't deserve for it to go well and for me to improve. I think it feels it won't be in control anymore. I am worried as to what will happen next if it feels threatened anymore."

As the therapy progressed, there was a remarkable change in her appearance. She wore dresses and was carefully made up. However, whenever the connectedness with the therapist was lost, she would revert to the quasimale image. It was as if when she was highly anxious, she was "occupied" by a male.

SOME THERAPEUTIC IMPLICATIONS

Kohut (1984) regarded his conceptions of *transmuting internalization* and the therapeutic error as central to his therapeutic method (see Chapter 17). The method depends on appropriate responses to disjunctions in the sense of connectedness between self and selfobject. It is essential, therefore, that the disjunction is detected. It is sometimes manifest as a reversal, which may be brief, perhaps indicated only in a phrase or single word. Following is an example:

The patient, who had spent much of his early life in an orphanage, could not remember anything before the age of 10. He begins the session by announcing that his girlfriend is pregnant. This appears to be "no problem" since she will get an abortion. After a few connecting sentences, the patient, showing little affect, goes on to say that he wonders if some early memories are beginning to be

recovered since he has had "images" of himself as a terrified child
being dragged from under a bed, presumably to be taken to the
orphanage. The therapist then remarks that the forthcoming
abortion seems to have triggered feelings relating to his having
been "got rid of" by his own mother. The patient says "good point"
in a rather pompous voice. He then recounts successive incidents,
without any apparent reason, in which he has been physically
attacked and injured, humiliated after revelation of an emotional
state, feeling paranoid, enraged.

The disjunction is signalled by the momentary reversal indicated by the authoritarian voice. There is a swift and transient
change. The therapist's response is sensed as an intrusion, threatening a precariously held inner zone, in the manner of a paranoid
system (Meares 1988). The therapist, however, failed to notice the
change of voice at "good point" and the session, afterwards,
seemed to lose its way.

A second important reason for the need to detect a reversal is
implied in the concept of *intersubjectivity* (Stolorow, Brandchaft,
and Atwood 1987). The reversal has an effect on the therapist, of
which he or she may be unaware. It creates a disruption that
causes the therapist's behavior to change. The language becomes
less impersonal (Meares 1983) and begins to focus on fact or
reason rather than the more emotional and inner aspects of the
patient's experience. A further disjunction is now inflicted upon
the patient. Our tapes show that in the treatment of those with a
very attenuated and precarious sense of self, a spiral, reminiscent
of the persecutory spiral is now set in train.[2] It may culminate in
a relatively fixed reversal in which the person who presents her-
or himself to the therapist seems relatively mature. The conversation that ensues may appear to be useful and adaptive but, in
fact, is going nowhere.

The notion of the relatively fixed reversal leads to another of
the therapeutic implications of the concept. The individual may
present in this state. Since the posture is frequently difficult to
recognize, there may be a long period of treatment in which
nothing can happen because the wrong person, as it were, is
being spoken with. This occurred with the patient described in
Chapter 8, whose main complaint was insomnia and an inability
to cope with even simple chores. She was treated behaviorally
without success. The patient's mother, so it seemed, had suffered

a posttraumatic stress disorder as a consequence of her experiences in World War II. This disorder results in severe problems with sleep, concentration difficulties, and a failure to cope. The therapist's first impression of the patient was of a little old eastern European lady, although she was only in her forties. It was only after some weeks had gone by that he realized that she had another voice, and indeed another appearance, which was charming and relatively vital. It seemed that, at first, she was inhabited by someone else.

Sometimes the patient is able to describe this kind of situation, sensing that his or her way of relating to others is not quite real. In this sense, it is one of the manifestations of a false self system (see Chapter 12). In extreme cases, such as the one described earlier in this chapter, the individual replicates his or her experience of someone else. In other cases, in which the original anxiety was presumably less, the individual seems to take on some of the functions of the failed selfobject. A variation of this phenomenon may be the so-called *grandiose false self*, in which the individual maintains a stance of arrogance and superiority of a brittle and unstable kind. This situation was described by Kohut (1971). "If the child suffers severe narcissistic traumas, then the grandiose self does not merge into the relevant ego content, but is retained in its unaltered form and strives for the fulfillment of its archaic aims" (p. 28). The compensatory aspect of this situation has been remarked upon by Stolorow and Atwood.[3]

A final implication concerns the possibility that reversals may sometimes be iatrogenic. There is a style of therapy in which interpretations are based on the idea that the patient's reality is disturbed by fantasy. Where the therapist's remarks are directed unremittingly at the unconscious, there is a danger that those with a fragile sense of self will have this precarious personal reality overthrown. Each interpretation has a strong potential to create a sense of disjunction. Where the patient's response unsettles the therapist, a *persecutory spiral* may develop. In the ensuing state of high anxiety, very little of the patient's self remains. The patient now takes in, in undigested form, a reality that is not his or her own. He or she becomes the other, even copying the therapist's mannerisms of speech and gesture. This dispiriting picture is the end point of a therapy, the falseness of which is unrealized by either partner.

SUMMARY

A reversal is the term applied to a fleeting change of self state in which the individual *becomes* the other. It is induced, in the first place, by intense anxiety, which obliterates inner reality. In the therapeutic situation, it is particularly likely to come about through a break in the connectedness between self and selfobject. This break, however, is experienced as massive compared with that produced by an optimal frustration in which the individual's sense of personal existence remains. When the break is optimal, a duality emerges, made up of an awareness of an inner life that contrasts with a response to it that does not fit and that is experienced as external. The reversal, in contrast, is adualistic.

In the therapeutic situation, a reversal is most likely to occur in those individuals whose sense of self is somewhat precarious, that is, in borderline personalities. An attenuated sense of self produces a vulnerability that may lead to a series of rapidly changing and often perplexing reversals during a single session.

Where the personality structure is more stable than that of the borderline, the reversal may become relatively fixed. In this case, it might be called an introject. Since it is surrounded by anxiety, it cannot be integrated into the self representation and remains relatively sequestered. Its adualistic basis fosters its fixity. Without reflection upon it, the system cannot change. The concept of reversal may be useful in the understanding of perpetrators of abuse, who have themselves been victims.

These pathological identifications are contrasted with those that are normal, anxiety-free, and that arise in a state of connectedness with another who is experienced as a selfobject. The word *internalization* might be used to refer to this process in order to distinguish it from introjection. The way toward healthy identification begins with the individual having within him or her the *dual* experience of both self and other. It is supposed that something like an oscillation goes on between these two poles, leading to an eventual integration of the experience of the other into the self representation so that its original form is no longer apparent.

Chapter 11 | STIMULUS ENTRAPMENT

We have so far considered people who in early life were constantly being made aware of the external world, who lived in an environment in which, ceaselessly, a reality that came from outside was forced upon them. This state of affairs culminates in a habitual state of experiencing, which I call *stimulus entrapment*. It is a form of disability that is often quite subtle, since it is not observed by those who do not know the individual well. Sometimes, indeed, he or she seems a model person, active, busy, very competent in those situations, such as committee work, in which linear thinking is important. When, however, such a person enters treatment for a prevailing sense of deadness, the true picture emerges.

The presenting picture is dominated by catalogs of events and of responses to stimuli. The patient talks endlessly of problems with the family, with work, and of bodily sensations. Nothing comes from an interior world. In essence, the patient seems unable to imagine.[1]

These people are truly trapped. They cannot relinquish the dependence upon stimuli, because if stimuli were to cease, nothing remains but a painful emptiness. As long as they go on seeking sensations, they are protected from it. But, in contrast, since they constantly seek stimuli, there is no opportunity to develop an interior zone. Indeed, as soon as life becomes relatively peaceful, distractions are sought that break up this relative calm. In some extreme cases in borderline patients, inexplicable crises develop when, for the first time, tranquility appears in their lives. Turmoil erupts as if it were needed. An alternative to turmoil is a preoccupation with bodily sensation.

The trap has reverberating consequences that compound the difficulty of escaping from it. Since there is no end to the impingements of the world, there is no silence[2] out of which can arise something that the person feels as his or her own. Yet an awareness of inner life allows others to connect with us. They can become selfobjects. When they do so, they allow a play space to emerge in which may be generated experiences sensed as peculiarly personal. A Catch-22 is apparent. Since connectedness with others as selfobjects cannot occur, inner life cannot come into being. Since inner life cannot develop, neither can connectedness occur.

The entrapment is further compounded by the effects of attention. It is part of ordinary experience that we enhance the intensity of a sensation by paying attention to it. For example, the physician listening to heart sounds, by extremes of attentional discipline, is able to hear what is normally not heard. An example of this capacity to magnify almost imperceptible stimuli is given by Levi-Strauss (1979). He discovered that before the era of navigational aids, sailors had developed extraordinary perceptual abilities. He found, through looking into old treatises on navigation, that the early mariners were able to see the planet Venus in full daylight, a feat that to the modern mind seems impossible. This kind of story provides a background to the growing body of evidence that suggests that attention has the effect of amplifying sensory input. In some cases, the effect of this amplification may reach the level of pain.

It seems clear that in a rough way, this magnification is reflected in the size of the electric potential wave evoked at the cerebral cortex by the stimulus. High intensity stimuli, including those that elicit pain, evoke large waveforms. The amplitude of the waveform, however, is not simply a function of stimulus intensity. It is altered by attention. It has been shown that the component of the waveform that arises about 200 milliseconds after the presentation of the stimulus can be increased by three times when the subject is asked to attend to the stimulus rather than ignore it (Miltner et al. 1989). One might predict that an extreme attentional focus upon ordinary bodily sensation may induce pain. This indeed seems to be the case. In one experiment, for example, subjects were connected to a sham stimulator and were told that a headache could occur as a result of the electrical current they received. This information might presumably cause at least some of the subjects to concentrate on inconsequential sensation in the head region. Half the subjects reported pain following this sham stimulation (Bayer et al. 1991).

Another mechanism of reverberation can now be seen to be contributing to the system of stimulus entrapment. Since sensation is necessarily fastened upon, its intensity increases, so enhancing the attention paid to it. This, in turn, helps to perpetuate the experience. Consequently, those who present in entrapment do not easily escape it. The conversation concerning events and symptoms can go on and on. Those therapists working according to the classical model report that it may persist for months, even years. The way out of the impasse is through the therapeutic relationship. The following case history from Kohut (1977) illustrates the effect of fluctuations in this relationship upon the individual's relative dominance by stimuli. It also introduces a further contributing factor to entrapment, that of anxiety.

> Mr. W. was periodically preoccupied by bodily sensations. In addition to his hypochondria, he suffered intermittent confusion, irritability, and a vague dissatisfaction with life. The periods during which he was markedly attentive to the stimuli coming from his body were more or less predictable. They occurred when he felt abandoned. This feeling was triggered by separations from those experienced as selfobjects. Early in the analysis, emotional distance or lack of empathy on the part of the therapist had the effect of a miniature separation, so that sessions were filled with "more or less anxious descriptions of various physical sensations he was experiencing and accounts of illnesses he believed he was suffering." [p. 155]

The anxiety that Kohut notes and that arises through separation or lack of connectedness with others who usually function as selfobjects is a fundamental aspect of the system of stimulus entrapment. It has long been known that anxiety enhances the intensity of stimuli and exacerbates the experience of pain. The pathophysiology of this phenomenon is not understood, but clinical evidence suggests that at a certain level of anxiety, a notional gating mechanism limiting the amount of sensory input, is breached (Melzack and Wall 1982). The consequence is an increased salience of stimuli. Kohut (1977) describes this. He notes that "the choice of symptoms during these episodes is not determined by specific unconscious wish fantasies . . . but pre-existing minor physical defects to which the patient paid little attention when the cohesion of his self was not threatened became the foci of his attention when his self began to fall apart" (p. 156).

The mood of diffuse anxiety, often experienced as a low grade tension, which follows the break with the selfobject, makes the loss of connection difficult to restore. Since the anxiety causes stimuli to be more intense, they are now also more salient. They have the effect of orienting the individual toward them so that inner experience cannot be generated. Since the therapist depends upon a resonance with his or her patient's inner states in order to create the selfobject experience, the disconnectedness must persist. The difficulty of getting started again after the break with the selfobject is implied in Kohut's description. The patient seems to be on strike against analysis. The analyst feels bored and conceives the block in terms of resistance. There is apparently nothing to be done that can overcome the atmosphere of stagnation.

During this period when the patient and therapist cannot connect, the therapist often comes to feel that the patient does not experience him or her as being in the room. The patient talks as if the therapist were simply not there. This feeling, however, is not accurate because the patient is so sensitized to stimuli that the smallest movement or inflection of voice is noticed. The patient's experience of the therapist is almost the opposite of the selfobject experience, as noted in an earlier chapter. Rather than being an extension of the subject's inner life, the therapist is totally outer. He or she is an extension of the patient's experience, which is almost entirely of the external world.

The chronic orientation toward external stimuli during this period of disconnectedness has the effect of amplification, as previously described. Their intensity increases. The individual begins to display unusual sensitivity to the sensory environment. Kohut (1977) describes in detail Mr. W.'s overreaction to strong sensory stimuli and the apparent "inability of his mental apparatus to handle the stimuli intruding from the surroundings and to cope with external problems of average complexity" (p. 163).

Although attention to stimuli is to some extent involuntary, in that it is a consequence of anxiety induced by the loss of the selfobject experience and by amplification, there is another force directing attention that is voluntary. The concentration upon physical sensation operates as a kind of defense. Its purpose is to evade an experience akin to annihilation. It seemed that Mr. W. used this attentional defense in childhood. During periods when his sense of self was threatened, he would pay particular attention to his body. He would lie awake for hours and make imagined "long excursions on his body. Starting from his nose, he would imagine himself walking over the landscape of his body down to his toes, then back again to his navel, shoulder, ear, etc.; thus reassuring himself that his body had not fallen apart" (Kohut 1977, p. 159). The busy concentration upon physical phenomena presumably had some soothing effect.

Mr. W. carried into adult life this means of calming himself. During a period of gross disconnection, he began to give an inventory of the items in his trouser pocket – the exact number of coins, a piece of crumpled-up notepaper, a small ball of woolly fuzz he had preserved, and so on. The therapist was struck by the quiet calmness of his voice. It was this element of the story that Kohut focused on and that enabled him to postulate that Mr. W.'s apparently resistant behavior was an antidote to self-fragmentation.

We are now led to another aspect of stimulus entrapment that concerns transitional phenomena. The break with the selfobject not only induces an orientation toward outer events and stimuli, but, on occasion, stimulates attempts to retrieve a sense of self through finding again, in a symbolic way, the lost selfobject. Sometimes these attempts involve perverse sexual activity (Meares 1990). Others, however, are far less obvious. An example is presented in Chapter 17 by a man who would talk in a boring way about motorcycle parts during those periods in a session when he sensed a disjunction between himself and his therapist. Tinkering with machines evoked memories of calm. This experi-

ence, it seemed, still adhered to motorcycles, which in this sense
had transitional qualities. In Mr. W.'s case, it was when the
therapist focused on the possible positive aspects of his inventory
that a connectedness was reestablished. Memories emerged that
pointed to the transitional nature of the apparently trivial things
that made up his catalog. Kohut (1977) recounts these memories
in the following way:

> . . . a number of childhood memories began to emerge concerning
> the time when he was first on the farm, when no one had paid
> attention to him, and when he was often alone while everyone was
> working in the fields. It was at such times, when his unsupported
> childhood self began to feel frighteningly strange to him and began
> to crumble, that he had in fact surrounded himself with his
> possessions—sitting on the floor, looking at them, checking that
> they were there: his toys and his clothes. And he had had at that
> time a particular drawer that contained his things, a drawer he
> thought about sometimes at night when he could not fall asleep, in
> order to reassure himself. His preoccupation with the contents of
> this drawer might well have been the precursor of his preoccupa-
> tion with the contents of his trouser pocket. [pp. 167–168]

This story shows us a possible way out of stimulus entrapment.
It suggests that the preoccupation with the physical world,
including the body, is not always random. Where the choice of
attention relates to past experience and has a certain meaning for
the patient, the therapist has the chance of making contact, albeit
limited, with the individual's personal reality. These connections
are initially small and quickly lost. Patience and resilience on the
part of both partners are required.

A persisting state of stimulus entrapment is accompanied by
low grade anxiety and tension in the patient, which is communi-
cated to the therapist, who may feel a sense of unease and
discomfort. The experience for the patient is not only a shrunken
innerness but also an attenuated sense of ownership and continuity of self.

As Goldberg (1983) has remarked, privacy and ownership are
two of the central themes apparent in the evolution of self. The
origins of a sense of ownership of experience are likely to be
complex. They will include the emergence of the play space, in
which the objects of play are those the child has chosen and that

represent his or her own experience in the way the child wishes. In contrast, experience coming from the external world does not have the quality of being owned. This notion, that experience coming from outside is not felt to be part of the personal system, whereas that which comes from within is felt as one's own, was noted by Descartes.

Descartes (1637–1641) tried to find the fundamentals of reality through introspective explorations. His purposes were ostensibly philosophical, but they also seemed to involve a search for the basis of self. Having locked himself away from all sensation, he described the ideas that came to him. They were, broadly speaking, of two kinds, some coming from "outside and yet others to have been made and invented by me. For the faculty which I have of conceiving what is called in general a thing, or a truth, or a thought, seems to me to derive from nowhere else than my own nature; but if I now hear a noise, if I see the sun, or if I feel heat, up to now I have judged that these sensations came from certain things existing outside me" (p. 116).

There are several consequences of a habitual mode of experiencing that come from "certain things existing outside me." Where experience comes from one's own nature, to use the words of Descartes, they are felt as peculiarly personal. These inner states have about them a state of "me-ness," which Claparède described in a classic paper written in 1911. He wrote: "The propensity of states of consciousness to cluster round a *me* which persists and remains the same in the course of time, is a postulate of psychology, as space is a postulate of geometry" (p. 67). These experiences are one's own. William James (1892) remarked that for most of us the elementary psychic fact is "not *thought* or *this thought* or *that thought*, but *my thought*, every thought being *owned*" (p. 153). For those caught in entrapment, however, whose experience comes from outside and so belongs to everyone, this sense of ownership of experience is lost.

An example is provided by a man who felt he was not quite alive. Although very successful, his ordinary experiences did not feel genuinely his own and lacked the quality of reality. Intuitively, he had come to the idea that an activity that in important respects was like a child's play, in this case writing, might be helpful. But it was not. What he produced did not feel as if it came from the core of him. Indeed, he wondered if it were anything more than a series of quotations from other people's work, that, inadvertently, he was a plagiarist. His story is very like a well-known case of Melitta Schmideberg.

> The patient was a scientist who was unable to publish, since he had a compulsion to plagiarize, for which he sought treatment. Ernst Kris (1951) took over this case and took the trouble to discover the content of the plagiarism. The man said he had just completed a book and had taken, despite himself, ideas from other people. In fact, the man had done nothing more than conform to the conventions of scientific writing in acknowledging and refer-encing his sources. Kris then made the interpretation that the patient wanted to be a plagiarist in order not to be one.
>
> Lacan (1977) reviewed this case and seemed, to my mind, to arrive at the right answer. "It's his having an idea of his own that never occurs to him" (p. 239). Put another way, the patient had never sensed that his ideas were his own and did not come from someone else.

Both these men, the scientist and the weekend writer, had been unable to develop an interior life that they felt as their own. A system of stimulus entrapment leads to a diminishment of a personal experience that is owned and unique, and to doubts about the authenticity of existence. Moreover, there is little confidence in the veracity of personal experience. This relative lack of confidence may extend to matters of simple and raw perception. This has been studied in an interesting experiment by Arnold Buss.

Buss (1980) devised a ten-item questionnaire that reflected private self-consciousness. The responses to this questionnaire given by normal people showed that there is a considerable variation in this parameter. Those whose evolution of an interior life was well developed were surer of their own perceptions and less likely to have the reality of others thrust upon them. For example, in one study, subjects drank a peppermint-flavored liquid and rated the strength of the flavor. Then, a second drink was presented, and half the subjects were told that it was stronger than the first liquid. Subjects high in private self-consciousness (Highs) gave almost the same intensity ratings to the second drink, whereas those low in private self-consciousness (Lows) rated it as more intense. The rest of the subjects were told that the second drink was weaker. Again, the Highs hardly changed their ratings at all, but the Lows rated the second drink as much weaker. Thus the Highs were not susceptible to suggestions about their taste reactions, but the Lows were.

These findings suggest that the development of an interior life brings with it a certain stability and continuity. Where, in contrast, innerness is lacking and the subject is stimulus dominated, personal reality is shifting, determined by others and, in this sense, discontinuous. Indeed, the lack of continuity of personal experience of those caught in stimulus entrapment is often remarkable. There is often no connection between sessions or even experiences in a particular session.

This system of enslavement to external circumstances is, in some individuals, extended beyond a lack of the sense of ownership of experience to an experience of falseness—the subject of the next chapter.

Chapter 12 | **FALSE SELF**

$\mathbf{M}$ost people caught up in the false self system do not seem false to others. This is one of its mysterious aspects. It is the people themselves who complain that their existence is fake, whereas those around them may see a lively and engaging but in no way fraudulent person. This state of affairs is illustrated by my first meeting with a young woman who was referred because her depression seemed intractable and had not responded to long courses of antidepressant medication. Apart from this, I knew only that she was a successful engineer.

> The first impression was surprising. She smiled and walked into the room with a step that was firm and decisive. Her dress was simple and stylish. She looked well. In following meetings she emerged as extremely likeable—quick, amusing, and charming. However, she experienced herself as unauthentic, saying such things as: "I copy people. I'm just an act, like being a fake person. I don't know what's really me." Or, "I take on other people's mannerisms on the telephone, so that others know who I'm speaking to. I'm worried about having no shape or form unless other people provide it. It's not legitimate for me to have opinions.

My personality is a facetious parodying of other people. I only exist in a negative way, reacting to other people."

Indeed, it was true that her attractive demeanor belied an underlying despair that broke through at times, as if it had little connection with the person who contained it. Quite unexpectedly at our first meeting, she began to cry in a way she could not explain. She could not be certain if she was crying through sadness and if this were so, from whence it came. She simply described an overwhelming sense of hopelessness, which came in almost formless waves. It was without images and there were no suitable words to attach to it.

This description was then interrupted by a brighter, firmer voice, which said, "It's getting on my nerves. I get fed up with this." Then followed, "I'm wondering why you should want to hear about this. Nobody likes to hear this kind of thing." She went on to say, "It means I'm not likeable. I don't like people seeing me like this."

This woman's conversation had two voices. One voice spoke of her misery; the other told her, in effect, to stop speaking in this way, that it was "getting on her nerves." The second voice sounded like a parent, in the manner of a reversal. The two voices suggested the possibility that as a child any expression of misery or distress would not have been tolerated. She would have been unlikeable. The sanction against this was presumably some withdrawal on the part of parents, a withdrawal frightening enough for the child to feel that it was safer not to experience those emotions, to somehow act over the top of them, and, if possible, ignore them.

In this way she gave up her own experience in favor of what was acceptable and what came from outside. She described a very difficult background—a father with a chronic illness, a vain and self-centered mother who was also probably depressed. The patient, however, was a brave and determined child. She learned not to complain of discomfort or even to experience it. For example, she suffered a hairline fracture of a bone in her forearm, but this was not discovered for days or weeks until a teacher noticed that something was wrong. Looking back, she could remember little pain. Other elements of her account suggested that she also learned not to recognize hunger or tiredness since a tired or hungry child might be bothersome to a parent.

Her story reminded one of a particular kind of delightful child whom Winnicott (1948) encountered from time to time. "The point about her is a vivacity which immediately contributes something to one's mood, so that one feels lighter. One is not surprised to learn that she is a dancer or to find that she draws and paints and writes poetry" (p. 92). What is important about her demeanor is that it is designed to enliven. It has the function of helping the mother through lifting her mood: "The mother's need for help in respect of the deadness and blackness of her inner world finds a response in the child's liveliness and colour" (p. 93).

Of course, it is not always the case that such a child, although enmeshed in her mother's moods, grows to be false. She may not obliterate her own experience in order only to show what the mother needs. Her capacity for enlivenment may come from something that is genuinely hers and that she may later contribute to larger groups, perhaps as a singer or an artist. Her life has been shaped rather than stifled. However, the young engineer was not so fortunate, for stiflement and deadness were what she habitually felt.

Her sense of the ownership and even the value of her experience and actions was diminished. For example, she felt she had messed everything up at work and considered whether to give it up. Yet she had just been awarded a prize by her Institute. It meant very little to her. She went on to say that she could not tell what was important, she could not assess her own standards and was unaware of how well she was performing. This related to her inability to tell whether, at times, she was happy or unhappy.

In a subtle way her existence was relatively discontinuous. She could not make links between her moods and events in her life. For example, when it was pointed out that a wave of misery seemed to follow a terrible argument with her sister, her reply was matter of fact. She accepted that there was a chronological relationship between the two events, but she was not at all sure that the link was causative.

Winnicott (1960), more than anybody else, drew attention to the system that underlies this woman's experience. Although, as he pointed out, he did not introduce the idea, he is seen as the principal theorist and proponent of the false self concept. He helps us to understand the patient's sense of the inauthenticity of personal experience, which on the face of it is not entirely logical. As the engineer remarked, "How can I say that I think what I feel isn't real? It is what I feel, it's all that there is, so it must be real."

Winnicott solves this puzzle by finding that what is real resides in the body. The argument necessarily begins with the experiences of early life.

The earliest and most fundamental experiences are bodily. There are presumably no affects that are separate from visceral, muscular, and dermal sensations. Psyche and soma are not distinguished. The core of self is bodily. The baby's feelings are spelled out, as it were, in bodily expression. The ordinary mother who behaves naturally reads them and responds. In this way she becomes something like an extension of the baby's own system. In this sense she is an illusion, as we have seen. She allows the baby to relate to her as an illusion. The illusion includes the child's belief that his or her wish, expressed in bodily movement or in other bodily ways, has brought about the response. Winnicott referred to this as *normal omnipotence.* He (1960) wrote of the baby's body expression as *the gesture* and of the way in which it maintains the illusion: "Periodically, the infant's gesture gives expression to a spontaneous impulse; the source of the gesture is the True Self, the gesture indicates the existence of a potential true self" (p. 145). When the mother responds to the gesture in a way that meets the affect it conveys, then "the true self has a spontaneity and this has been joined up with the world's events. The infant can now begin to enjoy the illusion of omnipotent creating and controlling" (p. 146). Put another way, the mother's response gives a shape, makes recognizable, what is going on in the baby's body. In this way, bodily states are joined up with emotions. Under these circumstances, the baby's emotional expression includes all the vitality of its bodily accompaniments. In (Winnicott's [1962]) favorable circumstances of the mother continuing to be "good-enough," the "skin becomes the boundary between the me and the not me. In other words, psyche has come to live in the soma" (p. 61). As time goes on, "the live body, with its limits, and with an inside and an outside, is *felt by the individual* to form the core for the imaginative self" (1949, p. 244). The circumstances, however, may not be favorable.

Two contrasting experiences of the mother are the forerunners or early prototypes of the two playrooms. Where the mother responds in a way that connects with the infant's subjective state, she is an illusion; where her response is not dictated by an immersion in the experiences of her baby, but is determined by her own concerns, she is real, the actual mother. When the response of the mother is of the latter kind, the baby is alerted and orients toward her. He or she is now aware of her, rather than him- or herself, showing an early form of other-directedness. There is consciousness now only of *her* gesture, which in this way is substituted in the baby's awareness for his or her own. A periodic awareness of response that comes from outside is necessary to maturation. Usually, the discrepant response does not break up those experiences that are early analogues of the field of play and in which the continuity of being is sensed. However, extreme maternal failure to adapt impinges on the baby like repeated loud noise. The embryonic self is, for these moments, obliterated. The infant can do nothing but react to stimuli that are alien. "In the extreme, there is very little experience of impulses except as reactions, and the ME is not established" (Winnicott 1950–1955, p. 217). If such a situation persists, there arises a need for impingements, since something must fill the gap where once was the continuity of being. Environmental impingement is a feature and must continue, "else chaos reigns, since the individual cannot develop a personal pattern" (p. 212). We enter now the zone of stimulus entrapment. Rather than a false self, what is being evolved to this point is a nonself. Through a hypertrophy of a dialogue with the real, "the individual then develops as an extension of the shell rather than the core, and as an extension of the impinging environment" (p. 212).

The next stage, the development of falsity, is a consequence of dependence. The child senses that existence depends upon a continuing bond with the parents. The child will do anything to maintain the bond, even to the extent of sacrificing his or her reality. In addition to responding unempathically, the mother may in various subtle ways demand particular responses from her child. For an anxious child, very slight changes in the mother, a frown, a turning away, may signify that the bond is about to be broken. The child searches for an indication of what the mother wants. He or she learns to emit certain behaviors in order to keep some link with the mother. This child not only reacts to stimuli but also complies with demands. A sense of falseness arises through a dislocation from bodily experience.

All normally developing children respond at times to implicit demands and behave in a way that complies with the wishes of others. This is an aspect of learning to live with others and of growing to become part of a social group. What is important, however, in the development of a false self is that the demand concerns emotional behavior. The child, for example, must appear to be happy. In giving this appearance, he or she is not giving expression to a feeling that encompasses the whole self, including the body. The life and vigor of the bodily accompaniments of an emotion are not experienced. What is expressed has, for the individual, something lacking in it. It has no sensorimotor aliveness. The woodenness and lack of vitality, which are the result of having to grow up under such domination, may be apparent to others, but frequently it is the individual him- or herself who feels that he or she is not "real," since a person's reality is based on body experiences. The words of emotional expression come from what the individual reads in the other's face rather than the assessments of his or her own physiology. The individual who has grown up in this situation ceaselessly scans the social environment in order to judge the expectations of others. One finds one's face being endlessly searched and small nuances of expression responded to.

In summary, the kind of false self discussed in this chapter is based upon compliance to the reality of the other. It is fueled by the belief that existence depends upon maintaining a bond with attachment figures. The result is not a mask. The function of the compliant false self is not to hide inner states, but to show those emotional expressions that will excite a suitable response from the other. The individual might describe him- or herself as a chameleon. The consequence of this behavior is that areas of personal experience remain neglected, never having been responded to. They stay sequestered and underdeveloped. No words attach to them. Often, they are sensed as formless, connecting with nothing. Other experiences that are expressible, involving words, images, and feelings, cannot be revealed since they threaten the link with the other. They form a system that cannot be elaborated since true interchange with the environment has ceased. Nevertheless, they may be sensed as a core of self—a limited self that cannot be enlivened or grow but remains static and repetitive. The individual's experience is now divided into two zones, the private and the public, which do not connect (Winnicott 1952).

There is no intermediate zone. The realization of this gulf between one's own thoughts and feelings and the world of others, and also the fear that it may be unbridgeable, is desolating. The sense of loneliness is profound. Therapy is directed toward allowing this secret zone of experience to emerge. As Winnicott (1974) put it: "Even in the most extreme case of compliance and the establishment of a false personality, hidden away somewhere there exists a secret life that is satisfactory because of its being creative and original to that human being. Its unsatisfactoriness must be measured in terms of its being hidden, its lack of enrichment through experience" (p. 80).

Chapter 13 | THE MASK

There is a second kind of false self system that is more truly masklike than that of compliance. In this case the individual feels that his or her existence depends not so much upon others, but upon the core experiences that must not be lost, damaged, or contaminated (Meares 1976). Winnicott (1963) came across this notion in a personal way. At the beginning of a paper on communication, he wrote:

> Starting from no fixed place I soon came, while preparing this paper for a foreign society, to staking a claim, to my surprise, to the right not to communicate. This was a protest from the core of me to the frightening fantasy of being infinitely exploited. In another language this would be the fantasy of being eaten or swallowed up. In the language of this paper, it is *the fantasy of being found.* [p. 179]

His response is perhaps different only in degree to that of the woman described in Chapter 1, who found the day difficult to get through because all interpersonal encounters seemed to involve something being demanded of her. Something of her precarious innerness had to be shown to others. It was as if Winnicott had been asked by the San Francisco Psychoanalytic Society to reveal his secret life. Pondering his response, he went on to remark:

> Ignoring for the moment still earlier and shattering experiences of failure of the environment-mother, I would say that the traumatic experiences that lead to the organization of primitive defenses belong to the threat to the isolated core, the threat of its being found, altered, communicated with. The defence consists in a further hiding of the secret self, even in the extreme to its projection and to its endless dissemination. Rape, and being eaten by cannibals, these are mere bagatelles as compared with the violation of the self's core, the alteration of the self's central elements by communication seeping through the defences. For me this would be the sin against the self. [p. 187]

As we have seen, the ideas, feelings, and memories that form this central core of existence are experienced as if they were substantial, so that any sense of damage to them is felt in an almost bodily way. A therapist who intrudes upon them or who invalidates or contaminates them takes on a persecutory aspect (Meares and Hobson 1977).

Winnicott spells out the dilemma that arises from his intuitions and that has been described earlier in this book. The individual needs intimacy but fears the damage that may result from exposure of what is innermost and generally kept secret. The developing individual needs to have something of his or her life remain secret. Intrusion into this area precipitates the defense of a masklike false self. Kohut (1977) described the difficulties experienced by the children of psychoanalysts. Although "good" parents, the psychoanalysts were too understanding. They assumed too much knowledge of their child's interior states. The response was a walling off of private life so that it became relatively inaccessible. An emotional distancing was set up. Rather than compliance, a kind of stubbornness becomes a feature of this personality. The mask is truly to ward off intrusion, which may be felt in the bodily and physical sphere, as well as in the psychical. An example was provided by a 30-year-old accountant who lived with a woman with whom he refused to have sexual relations. It seemed that this was related to a fear of intrusion of others into his inner space. The places where he lived became metaphors of the inner world. For example, the patient insisted on the privacy of his study, and he would become enraged if he discovered that his books had been moved around. He tried to keep her out in many ways, so that when his companion talked to him, he would continue another train of thought in his head as if to exclude her from his own experience. If she asked him to do some chores, he would fail to carry out her wishes, since it seemed as if he was being ordered around and, in this way, being made her own.

Some, at least, of the origins of his fear were to be found in the behavior of his mother who, in many ways, was gentle and well-meaning but who was also very immature. She intruded upon him in many ways. For example, when he was young, she reversed their roles. Rather than allowing her child to chatter and play while she encouraged both with her presence and responsiveness, she usurped his position. It was she whose chatter fastened on the passing events of the world around her in an incontinent way: "Look at that . . . come and see this," and so on. It was she who found the beetle and the strangely colored leaf. Moreover, the child was never allowed out of her sight. Superficially, the appearance was of a good mother, concerned and preoccupied with her child. Her effect, however, was of gross intrusion upon the child's developing sense of self. His responses included attempts to establish his own autonomy so that she found him difficult. At times, he would have rage attacks. Her disregard of boundaries continued into his twenties so that, as if they were husband and wife, she would urinate in front of him or embrace him like a lover.

This kind of story illustrates the effect of intrusion into the private core of self. As a matter of survival the individual begins to adopt a posture that keeps others away from this area of experiencing. Intrusion, however, is a minor trauma compared with those responses that diminish the value of that which is most inner, most intimate, and often concerned with the tender emotions. When the developing person reveals something of this core and it is mocked or in other ways denigrated, the blow is followed by hatred. The *malevolent transformation* (Sullivan 1953), now comes into being. The individual is unlikely to allow such damage to occur again. He distances himself from others so that what is inner cannot be known. Although conducting day-to-day conversation and operating among others, this person has become an isolate, in whom lingers a lasting sense of hidden rage and desire for revenge.

The strategies adopted to maintain the integrity of the inner core are many. Distancing, silence, and withdrawal are characteristic. Rather than compliance, as previously remarked, noncompliance is a feature of the intruded-upon individual. An incident, described in more detail elsewhere (Meares 1976) illustrates this attitude. A boy whose secret was the biography of a murdered queen spent his free time gathering information about her and visiting the places she had lived. On one occasion he cut passages from library books that referred to her. This caused him to be charged with an offense against public property. In court, he obstinately refused to utter one word of defense or explanation. He simply stared out a window as the magistrate questioned him. The matter was his own personal and sacred mystery, not to be sullied by the legal process.

The core, as this incident suggests, often consists of a series of images relating not only to who-one-is, but also to the mother or mother–child dyad, who are symbolically represented. These central images are highly charged, invested with an emotional tone that might be called libidinal.[1] Indeed, ideas or fantasies of a sexual kind are an important part of this central constellation.

We have so far considered the false self system that protects an inner core as distinct from what is designed to maintain the bond with others. The two systems, however, often combine. Yukio Mishima, in his 1958 novel *Confessions of a Mask,* describes such a situation. The central character is a homosexual, a fact that cannot be revealed in the society in which he lives. In addition to hiding his sexual fantasies, the hero tries to comply with the wishes of his family. He pretends to fall in love with a girl. As a result, his own experience is lost or, at least, he is uncertain of what is his own.

> My "act" has ended by becoming an integral part of my nature, I told myself. It's no longer an act. My knowledge that I am masquerading as a normal person has even corroded whatever of normality I originally possessed, ending by making me tell myself over and over again that it too was nothing but a pretense of normality. To say it another way, I'm becoming the sort of person who can't believe in anything except the counterfeit. But if this is

true, then my feeling of wanting to regard Sonoko's attraction for me as sheer counterfeit might be nothing but a mask to hide my true desire of believing myself genuinely in love with her. So maybe I am becoming the sort of person who is incapable of acting contrary to his true nature, and maybe I do really love her. [p. 153]

The result is similar to that of compliance. Slowly the inner reality fades and the individual's responses and behavior, which were once a pose, now seem *as if* they were real, to use the term of Helene Deutsch.

The two kinds of false self system described here do not exhaust the possibilities. A third category, which arises in a way that resembles the system of reversals, must be briefly touched upon. Consider the following.

A woman of 35 is being seen for the first time. She has been referred because she has had difficulty in sleeping recently and has been drinking heavily. Her appearance conforms to the stereotype of the actress. She is noticeably bejeweled, expensively dressed, and carefully made up. Her manner is both patronizing and charming. She suggests that nothing is really wrong. It is simply that her sleep has been poor since breaking up with her fiancé. Perhaps some medication can fix it?

The therapist responds in the manner of the physician, telling her that any therapeutic suggestion must be based on a thorough knowledge of the details of her life. Since he does not respond to the central element of her story—the difficulty in soothing herself—nor to the anxiety she is experiencing in the present, a disjunction occurs. She suddenly becomes quite grandiose—angry, arrogant, and contemptuous. This grandiosity has a fakeness about it. It is a posture.

The grandiose false self, in which the subject takes on aspects and functions of the other who has failed, is part of the fluctuating picture of the so-called narcissistic personality. Its obvious inauthenticity and defensive quality sometimes causes others to challenge it or confront it. A further disjunction then occurs and the grandiose stance becomes more pronounced. A much less obvious and more socially acceptable version of this kind of false self Winnicott called the *caretaker self*. This element of the personality is competent and sensible and, as it were, brings the patient along for treatment. Winnicott (1960) describes the situation in the following way:

In analysis of a False Personality the fact must be recognized that the analyst can only talk to the False Self of the patient about the patient's True Self. It is as if a nurse brings a child, and at first the analyst discusses the child's problem, and the child is not directly contacted. Analysis does not start until the nurse has left the child with the analyst and the child has become able to remain alone with the analyst and has started to play. [p. 151]

Winnicott did not elaborate upon this scenario, which he uses as his main example of the false self in his classic essay on the subject. Although it has similarities to the systems of compliance and hiddenness, it differs from them. It corresponds more closely to the phenomenon of reversal, but is not identical with it. Whereas the reversal depends, in extreme cases, upon a replication of the other, the phenomenon of the caretaker self involves taking on necessary functions and attitudes of the caregiver who has failed. Finally, Winnicott (1960) suggested that there is a "normal" false self system, manifest as ordinary politeness. Is this the case? I do not think so.

There can never be an exact equivalence between self, as interior life, and identity or who-one-is-for-others. One has to do largely with thoughts, feelings, images, whereas the other has to do with behavior. The translation from one to the other cannot produce a replica. Nevertheless, where the inner zone of thought and feeling and the outer one of behavior coexist, so that one lives largely in the intermediate zone of Winnicott, then falseness is not experienced. Where, however, the social manner is based on the desire for acceptance by a particular group, so that behavior loses touch with inner experience, a false self emerges, which consists of a fashionable façade. It is a variant of the system of compliance.

In conclusion, three kinds of false self have been described.[2] Each exists in relatively pure form, but the elements of compliance, hiddenness, and compensation are often mingled. A lack of true interchange between inner experience and the outer world is common to them, so that the area of real and bodily living has become shrunken. The sense of the reality of experience, its connection with the body's aliveness, is lost. The result is a persisting feeling of deadness, boredom, and dissatisfaction.

Part III | **RESTORATION**

Chapter 14 | BEGINNING AGAIN

The cardinal features of the borderline syndrome are deadness, emptiness, and low self-esteem; rapidly fluctuating moods and sense of self; an inability to be alone amounting to an addiction to certain people, events, and even to stimuli; periodic experiences akin to annihilation and fragmentation; impulsive and apparently maladaptive behaviors. At the heart of these disturbances lies the fear that there is "no real me." This constellation of experiences and behaviors can be understood in terms of the outline of the development of self and its disruption, given in previous chapters. A more extended catalog of the features of severe personality disorder appears in the notes. These features are briefly related to the model I have described.[1] Now, we approach the problem of treatment.

Someone who has been so impinged upon in early life that in adulthood shows the stigmata of personality disorder has suffered a developmental arrest. As Jung (1954) put it: "Certain parts of the personality which are capable of development are in an infantile state, as though still in the womb" (p. 9). Seen in this way, the therapeutic purpose is to begin again the developmental processes that were impeded in childhood. In 1935, Jung told a group of British psychotherapists that "analysis is a process of quickened maturation" (p. 172). Beginning again, however, is no easy task. It is not re-mothering as is sometimes imagined, since the signals upon which the ordinary, devoted, and "good-enough" mother depends are no longer present, or are used in a distorted way. The means of connection have been lost. Nevertheless, principles of development derived from observations of children are used in approaching those with disorders of self. In essence, the aim of the therapist is to create conditions in which a mental activity emerges that is analogous to that underlying the play of the 3-year-old child.

Since play occurs in an actual place, this is where we must start. This fact is not considered often enough. It is important to the task of psychotherapy in a way that hospital authorities, among others, frequently fail to recognize.

Because a history of impingement is the basis of the patient's disorder and because he or she is now unduly sensitive to intruding stimuli, it is important to reduce the salience of the environment. The place must be quiet, free of noises from the corridor, from telephones, and the sounds of conversation in neighboring rooms. This seems so obvious as to be banal. Yet hospital psychiatric services are rarely set up with these provisions in mind.

The decoration of the room should reflect something of the therapist, who is expected to be ordinarily human, and not the opaque, neutral individual of classical times. He or she lives like other people and has around him or her things that are personal. Nevertheless, his or her life should not obtrude. The therapist, after all, is attempting to become a facilitating background, to become impersonal in the same way that an artist is impersonal (Eliot 1932). That is, his or her own personality is not imposed upon what is being created.

Perhaps, however, the most important characteristic of the setting is reliability. The child must have confidence in a fairly predictable environment. It is only through such confidence that play can begin. Those with disorders of self are often extremely sensitive to small changes in the environment and are disturbed by them. The significance of this predictable environment has been noted earlier. It is as if this space becomes a precursor of inner space.[2] However, those who work in busy hospitals often have to use different rooms from week to week, unsettling their patients. Reliability in terms of space is often neglected in discussions of the therapeutic setting, whereas the therapist's temporal reliability is, rightly, emphasized.

The play space, however, is not purely physical. It depends upon a peculiar atmosphere that arises when a feeling of connection is established. Those, however, in whom the development of a sense of self has been disrupted are usually unable to make contact. The ways of connecting are blocked. What is offered is limited and may be a form of pseudo-contact. We have touched upon the reasons for this. Since what is inner is precarious and fragile, its revelation cannot be risked through fear of damage; alternatively since there is no sense of what is inner, true connection cannot occur. Perhaps all that can be offered is a system of compliance or of stimulus entrapment.

More often, the lack of connection is more subtle. The therapist, in trying to stay with the patient, responds to what is offered. Soon, he or she is caught up in the patient's system, somehow aware that nothing is happening but unable to lift him- or herself out of an interaction that is repetitive and in which both parties seem trapped.

A compounding difficulty is anxiety. The early conversations between therapist and patient may be accompanied by a low-grade tension, which is so much part of the background that it is barely noticed. It arises through the patient's habitual difficulty in connecting. Where engagement does not occur, the patient is in a state of disjunction. This disjunction breeds anxiety, which reverberates in the encounter, further reducing the chances of connection by impeding access to imaginative life. The patient and the other are now caught in a circular situation that it is often difficult to break out of (described in Chapter 11). When the sense of connection between patient and therapist begins, so also does a sense of relaxation. Alternatively, where the therapist has the capacity for relaxation, the chance of connectedness is enhanced.

The work toward connectedness begins in the first moments of the encounter. Indeed, the core of the patient's problem is often encapsulated in the opening few words and in his or her initial demeanor. Following are three examples of the first few minutes and their significance.

A young man walks into the room. He says nothing, but his eyes are wide and ceaselessly scan the therapist's face. It soon emerges that his mother was frequently drunk and unpredictable. The child learned to be acutely aware of minute changes in her expression, which might predict an outburst.

A woman of about 30 says brightly as she steps into the office: "What a nice sense of space." It seems a mere pleasantry, yet of the many people who have been in the office, I do not remember anybody else having made this remark, at least at first. Later in this first session, she explains that she is seeking treatment for a sense of stiflement, which she feels has been inflicted upon her by overprotective parents and then by a paternalistic husband. She seeks a sense of space where she can find herself and believes, at this stage, that this must come through leaving her husband.

A man of 50 says "good morning" politely as we shake hands. I know from the referring letter that he is a brilliant lawyer who has become depressed following his wife's leaving him for a mechanic. As he sits down, he asks: "Do you mind if I smoke?" "If you like," I reply. There is a slight pause. He says: "Some people would object you know." He is saying, obliquely, that in the eyes of some, a competent doctor would not permit smoking. Yet, my refusal would have been discourteous, a contrast to his own politeness. Either response will be wrong. I can only be rude or incompetent. A trap had been set. In these few words, the outlines of an interpersonal system are suggested. It was later confirmed. What worked in court had ruined his marriage. His wife could not tolerate the sense of being trapped and had to flee.

The opening is particularly important because it is likely to be relatively spontaneous and it is, as Winnicott remarked, the spontaneous gesture that reveals what is genuine and must be responded to. As the story begins to be told, the unrehearsed quality of the opening remarks is often lost. Something closes over. The story may give the impression of having been told before. The therapist must try to find more than is shown, or else connection will never occur.

The tone of voice, the face, the body movements may show more than the words of the conversation. The words, however, also suggest more than their overt meaning. They may be unobtrusive metaphors helping to portray the individual's psychic world. The therapist must listen to more than the information in the patient's story and must imaginatively consider the implication of the *exact* words and the precise expression that has been used. For example, a man talks about the fact that his girlfriend and he have decided to live together. He says she is "moving in." The choice of expression may be simply chance. Nevertheless, it invites speculations about the significance of intrusion. It must be clear that these are only speculations, providing the opportunity for exploration and elaboration.

The precise words and their load of multiple meanings are the preoccupation of the poet. It seems that poets and psychotherapists have, ideally, much in common. As a digression, I touch upon the effect of focusing upon the actual words in order to elaborate meaning beyond the bare bones of the patient's story. I use a simple poem, by "Banjo" Patterson, which tells a story and which is known to every Australian school child. It begins:

There was movement at the station, for the word had
    passed around
That the colt from old Regret had got away.

Let us consider these words and their effect. There was "movement." Why "movement?" It seems there is drama afoot. Why not use a word like "bustle" or "flurry" or "tumult" to convey the consternation at the escape of the valuable horse? At first sight, "movement" seems too slight. Yet when we think about it, it conveys a sense of vastness. It is as if we are somewhere in the sky, above the enormity of the Australian landscape. Down below, something is perceptible–"movement." We enter the region of the epic.

This effect is compounded in the next sentence–"the word had passed around." There are no men in it. The *word* has its own life, "passing around" from group to group, in the manner of the epic, living on beyond the people who made it.

Finally, "the colt from old Regret." She is not called Bullitt or Raspberry or Sara, but old Regret. Into the spatial vastness comes time, time lost, time passing. It is interesting that a poem constructed as if it were an epic has become one.

This diversion helps illustrate the value of pondering the use of particular words, of not losing sight of the actual text. This focusing, however, leads us to a paradox, many of which underlie the psychotherapist's stance. In addition to focusing, the therapist must be unfocused. Rather than fix attention on any one feature of his encounter with the patient, he or she must be aware of series of themes of sensations, perceptions, feelings, imaginings, and memories. He or she must maintain, as Sigmund Freud put it, "an evenly suspended attention."[3] This state includes the capacity to notice changes in one's self as the patient's story is being told and, as it were, to become a spectator to those experiences. Why is it, for example, that concentration is lost, unease is felt, or an uncharacteristic remark is about to be made? Above all, however, in his or her attempt to make connection, the therapist attends to feelings. When two people are together, their sense of harmony is based on feeling. The therapist connects with the patient through responses to peculiarly personal and emotional elements of the patient's communication. In order to do this, he or she must be listening for changes and nuances in the conversation that are based on spontaneous emotion. What is alive is immediate and found in the present. The past is useful and creative only when it is lived in the present.

Spontaneous emotion, as compared with emotion that is habitual and perhaps part of a false self system, offers the first steps toward setting up the enabling atmosphere analogous to that of the play space. When the therapist is able to respond in a way that shows an understanding of the most personal elements of what the patient has been saying, there is sometimes a marked change in the form of the conversation. Instead of moving in a straight line, the story takes unexpected turns, just as in play, and the language accompanying it moves in a capricious and wandering way. Moreover, the content of the conversation tends to become more emotional and personal. In the beginning, however, this deviation from a linear mode of speaking and experiencing is slight, merely a sentence or two, a transient flickering away from the previous path. A therapist who has seen this happen sometimes feels as if he or she has to "kick start" the session. Each time the session begins with the habitual sense of disconnection, and each time the therapist has to respond appropriately to a feeling state before anything can happen.

These tiny excursions into what might be called, in a metaphoric sense, the play space, are the beginning of therapy. An example of the effect of tracking the immediate conversation follows. The therapist stays very close to what she is given.

Robin was a 30-year-old woman who had grown up under extremely adverse circumstances, the consequence of which was the development of a false self system. All three forms of this system are operative, as we discover. This session occurred relatively early in the therapy. It took place in a busy general hospital. Because of an emergency call, the therapist, a young female psychiatrist, was 30 minutes late. The patient began in a pleasant and conversational tone.

> **Patient:** A lot of catching up to do, have you?
>
> **Therapist:** Yes—keeping me late. Mm.
>
> **Patient:** (Laughs in a sisterly and sympathetic way) You sound a bit winded.

[Given her patient's history of deprivation, the therapist knows that the patient will fear separation, even of the smallest degree, and as a consequence the nonarrival of her therapist will have made the patient anxious. Anxiety, however, is nowhere betrayed in these opening remarks. This suggests that Robin has learned that the expression of negative emotion is not tolerated by those around her. Not only is genuine expression unacceptable, it seems that she has to look after those whose role it is to look after her. She may feel the therapist is uncomfortable or even guilty over her late arrival. She responds to her therapist in a way designed to make her feel better.]

> **Patient:** (pause) I'd like to discuss what we discussed on Monday.
>
> **Therapist:** Mm.
>
> **Patient:** I can't remember what we did discuss. (She then laughs in an infectiously engaging way.) What were we discussing on Monday?

[The patient cannot remember what is unpleasant since it is unacceptable. She has learned to repress what the mother will not tolerate. She allows herself to experience only what is permissible. As a consequence she asks what went on during the Monday session. The therapist is encouraged to determine, even create, the patient's experience. In this way the relationship with the mother is recapitulated.

The patient enmeshed in a false self system is always trying to discover what the therapist wants.]

Therapist: Lots of things. Something's on your mind that related to Monday?

[The therapist avoids the pitfall of selecting the patient's experience. Instead she relates the patient's need to raise Monday's events to the patient's present state.]

Patient: Being accused of wasting money (by her husband). That really cut in. Mainly that that's bothering me. Feel really hostile.

Therapist: That is what you'd like to discuss?

[The feeling that is remembered from Monday is hostility. This relates to being misunderstood, albeit in a gross and derogatory way. It seems possible that this again relates to the present.]

Patient: Well, I don't often feel that angry. He started on me on Friday and didn't let up, constant pick pick picking over the weekend. Sometimes I just wish I had a place where I could go and not have anybody hassle me or even talk to me. Sometimes I can go 3 or 4 days without talking.

Therapist: To have your privacy.

[The therapist follows what is offered.]

Patient: Yes. Privacy is very hard to find in our house.

Therapist: You can't get privacy.

Patient: No. Even in the bath when you want to relax, the kids want something.

Therapist: People seem intrusive—sort of barge in.

[A new theme has arisen. It concerns the need for a sense of personal space in which one's own experience can, as it were, live and grow. Her desire for private experience, however, is constantly frustrated by her mother who is intrusive and dominating. Even now, although the patient is in her thirties, her mother is in constant contact with her. She is often in the patient's home, sometimes using the latter's bedroom to change her clothes. The bedroom is a place where the patient tries to express something of herself so that the mother's intrusion into this area is like a violation of intrapsychic space. In the bedroom is a poster of a rock star who dresses bizarrely, often in a way that suggests an ambiguity of sexual identity. This poster expresses aspects of Robin's identity, in particular, her gender identity. Even this fantasy is not allowed to remain as her own. Her mother cuts out newspaper articles about the rock singer and sends them to her daughter.]

Patient: It's taken for granted you're always there. They're always wanting me to do things, but whenever I want something done, nobody's ever got the time.

Therapist: So it seems unfair.

[The therapist's remarks seem simple, and in one sense they are. She is behaving naturally, rather like a mother, who without thinking about it, fits in with her child's experience. She responds to the momentary changes in the patient's mood, in this case the sense of the unfairness of others that is found in the tone of expression rather than Robin's actual words.]

Patient: I think it's unfair. Why should I always be there for somebody, but when I want somebody, nobody's there?

[This statement relates not only to the fact that throughout her life others have used her for their own needs and that she never complained or spoke out, but also, presumably, to the therapist's failure to be "there" at the expected time. The therapist has the opportunity of pointing this out. Put another way, she might offer a transference interpretation. Instead, she chooses something different. She tries to develop what seems to be most immediate in her patient's experience, which is expressed in her body.]

Therapist: And that's why you can't sit still?

[Body movements are likely to reflect genuine emotion and, in the case of someone who has spent a lifetime concealing her true feelings, to be closer to the heart of the personal than what is conveyed by words alone. Although the form of the therapist's verbal expression may be questioned, the effect of her intervention cannot. It very quickly leads to the patient's underlying emotional state.]

Patient: (laughs) Yeah. I have to be on the move all the time. (pause) Whenever I get really depressed, I get this really tight wound up feeling, that's why I keep moving (laughs loudly).

Therapist: Tight in your whole body, your stomach?

[The therapist tries to elaborate the experience, starting with its most primitive components—the bodily.]

Patient: Yeah (laughs rather nervously). I get a real pressure feeling at the back of the head. If I don't do something—jump up and down, scream or something—it feels as if the back of my head's going to blow off.

Therapist: This is when you feel depressed?

[The therapist's remark closely follows the text. The patient has already said that depression accompanies her body's tightness and feeling wound up. The therapist's assumption is that the expression of the emotion itself would have not been permissible during Robin's development and that only the somatic and concrete elements of the experience were acceptable. Reintroducing the word *depression* is an attempt to elaborate the feeling state.]

Patient: This is when I feel self-destructive (laughs loudly).

[The laugh, because it is quite engaging, is not obviously defensive. Yet that is what it is. Robin's fear of expressing depression is such that she does not admit to the state itself—only to those acts that might accompany it.]

Therapist: Self-destructive? What—overdoses or cutting your wrists?

Patient: Oh, I've only overdosed a couple of times. Sometimes when you think of o/d-ing, well, they can stomach pump you, but slashing your wrists is so final, isn't it? How long does it take blood to pump out of your body? About 6 minutes? Then you think of the kids—so there's this constant thing of the walls closing in all the time.

[This is a difficult connection. There seems to be a link between feelings of self-destruction (or depression) and a constriction of personal space as if one might be the result of the other.]

Therapist: Is that happening at the moment?

[The therapist again concentrates on immediate lived experience— what is happening now rather than at other times in other places. Once again her intervention connects.]

Patient: I feel very (laughs) closed in here. While I'm in here I can't look you in the eye. I'm always watching the walls (laughs very loudly). As I said, the door handle's right there, so . . . as long as the door's not locked (laughs).

[It is as if to look someone in the eye is to invite another to see into her inner world. This kind of intrusion is what she tries to avoid.]

Therapist: I wonder if the tightness and tension have something to do with us starting 30 minutes late.
Patient: Oh no, no. I have had this—it started building up since last Friday.
Therapist: Right.

[The therapist has obviously been waiting to introduce the subject of her lateness, since Robin's response to it will have been providing an important undercurrent of feeling during this dialogue. Perhaps the patient's rejection of her therapist's supposition is accurate. It is possible that the therapist has not directly taken from what was happening at the moment and has reverted to theory. It is, however, equally possible that Robin finds it difficult to accept negative feelings directed toward the other. The therapist, of course, is right in accepting Robin's rejection of her speculation.]

Patient: As if something's bound to happen.

[A sense of threat, a feeling that some disaster is about to occur, is characteristic of the anxiety that arises during separation. Although Robin has overtly rejected her therapist's attempt to approach the matter of her lateness, she now seems to be talking about it covertly.]

Therapist: That's what you feel? Something's going to go wrong, or you're going to do something, or . . .

Patient: Oh, something might go wrong. I don't really know how it's going to come out. I just ride with it and that. I don't know. I've tried to explain it to people. They sort of go "huh" (contemptuously)—everybody gets tense—fair enough, everybody probably does get tense. Rushing from up there down here thinking I mustn't be late—things like that. There's levels of depression.

[Here everything comes out in a rush and somewhat incoherently. She seems to be saying that those around her fail to understand her feelings and, indeed, do not wish to understand them. She implies that the therapist is part of this social universe. But at the very moment when she begins to express such a thought, she obliterates it. "Rushing from up there down here thinking I mustn't be late" represents a condensation of two opposite tendencies. The first is to connect the therapist with those who contemptuously dismiss her feelings of tension. The second, and much more powerful tendency, is to empathize with the therapist and to understand her hectic life and her anxiety. The impulse to take up the caretaker role, to look after the therapist, overwhelms her own experience.]

Therapist: What level now?

[There are many things in the previous passage that the therapist could follow. She has to make a choice. Since she is aware that Robin has adopted a mask of jolliness that hides her depression from others, and in this way perpetuates her sense of futility and worthlessness, the therapist picks out the depressive theme and at the same time tries to keep it in the present.]

Patient: I've been putting on a front for so long. It sometimes takes a while for me to realize that I'm alone there and something might happen.

[Robin acknowledges the mask. She also acknowledges that there were feelings relating to the therapist's lateness, but this is expressed obliquely—"I'm alone there" presumably refers to the waiting room. Third, and importantly, she seems to be saying that because of the mask she is no longer able to discern what her feelings really are, or at least, it "takes a while" for her to realize. This may explain Robin's initial rejection of the connection between tension and waiting.]

The session has now begun. Robin begins to talk in a way that is less focused on the therapist and the events of the outer world and turns to her own, inner universe. The conversation has a discursive form—various episodes of a personal nature being touched upon in an apparently random way. These episodes do not have logical connections. They are linked, however, by associations around a broad general theme. She talks of her girlfriend, who the previous day had failed to turn up for a coffee appointment; "She's whimsical" was Robin's explanation. The bathroom as a symbol of personal space is mentioned again; she describes more clearly the wish for someone to say "right, what's the matter," but nobody will.

The form of this kind of mental activity resembles play. It does not move in straight lines. It seems broken up. The seamless account of events in the outer world is replaced by a series of personal episodes, often very short.

This change is brought about by a therapist who is responsive to small degrees of change in the patient's emotional state. She is impersonal in that, as far as possible, she brings nothing of her own life into the engagement. Even theory is eschewed. Instead, she uses her sensitivity and imagination, saying very little, giving no explanations. She is not trying to be clever, as Winnicott put it.[4] She is merely trying to become attuned to her patient's experience. Attunement, however, is not enough. Indeed, unless there is progression beyond it, there is danger of a new system of entrapment arising, in which the therapist is merely an echo. In order for self to emerge, the therapist's response must ultimately have an effect that is beyond that of engagement and that participates in the elaboration of inner life.

Chapter 15 | MIRROR, MEANING, AND REALITY

The typical form of mother–infant interaction cannot be used as a direct guide to making an engagement with a person as damaged as Robin, discussed in Chapter 14, had been. Since her demeanor belies her underlying state, her entrapment is reinforced by the ordinary, natural responses of others. Nevertheless, the model of the proto-conversation, of Trevarthen's dance between mother and baby, does suggest certain principles of therapeutic behavior. We come to a complex form of responding, which has been called mirroring.

The young therapist working with Robin was, on the face of it, confronted with an insoluble dilemma. She knew that what her patient offered her as a means of intercommunication was false and should not be the basis of their conversation. Yet, she also knew that she *must* respond to it, since Robin depended upon her pleasant demeanor to make a bond with others. Without it she was plunged into anxiety. However, the therapist knew she had to speak to the person who, as it were, was hiding behind the attractive laugh and comforting facade. Her resolution of the dilemma, of which she was probably unaware, was to act as if she were double. This paradoxical stance introduces mirroring.

The therapist had a naturally engaging style. Through her face, her eyes, and non-specific remarks, she responded to the patient's public persona while at the same time trying to hear the frightened, sad, and angry person who could not present herself. Once again, we find the therapist being required to develop a paradoxical stance. The therapist is doing two things at once. Through her generally approving demeanor, she was, to a limited degree, mirroring, at the same time tracking the moment-to-moment changes in the patient's experience. In very broad terms, Robin emitted false positive emotional signals through her smiling and laughing while involuntarily concealing negative affect. This division of affective life into positive and negative helps to introduce the subject of mirroring.

The mother responds in different ways to the two categories of affect. If the baby is distressed, the mother does something about it. If the baby is crying through hunger, it is fed; if the child is frightened, he or she is comforted. The task of the mother, on these occasions, is to understand her child and to respond according to her understanding. The therapist's purpose is similar. However, the task is more difficult since the signals have been altered, so that understanding is not always simple and natural, as it is for the mother. It involves concentration and even discipline. We return to this activity in the following chapter.

The mother's behavior when the baby's emotional state is positive differs from what she does when the baby is, for example, frightened or unhappy. When the baby's affect is positive, the mother often participates and contributes to it. Her behavior has an imitative element and in this way it is unlike her response when the baby is distressed. She does not, for example, mimic his crying (although she may frown and even moan a little bit). However, when the baby's affect is positive, the mother's response is characteristically to mirror it. When the infant is content, for example during feeding, the mother is content; when the child is interested, she too shows interest; when the child is happy, the mother behaves like the child, escalating the happiness.

This mirroring response, as we have seen, has at least two important elements. The first involves a reciprocal positivity, which, at its least intense, involves an attitude of interest and implicit approval on the part of the mother. At an extreme, there arises an atmosphere of idealization, which from the parent's side is akin, as Kohut put it, to child worship (Elson 1987).

The second important aspect of mirroring is the representation of the other's personal experience. The earliest representations are made by the responsive caregiver's face and voice, which reflect and echo the baby's emotional state. The expression on the mother's face is equivalent to a word. Her response is analogous to naming the formless experience that inhabits the baby. She gives it a reality.

At first, the naming or representing of the baby's experience goes on face to face. There is no other reality than that which is instinctive and bodily. Soon, however, there is a movement of attention toward what the baby is doing and expressing in action. Instead of the original dyad, the engagement now has three components—the third is the baby's activity, which is directed toward the environment. In this new, tripartite situation, the caregiver's naming or representing continues. This is illustrated by the Sorce and Emde experiment noted in Chapter 5 (Sorce et al. 1985). They studied children aged about 1 year. Each child was placed on the shallow side of the so-called visual cliff. The mother was on the other side and the baby crawled toward her. At some point, as the child moved out across the glass, he or she became aware of the increasing space below. The child glanced up at his or her mother in order to discover the meaning of this strange situation in which he or she was poised, apparently precariously, over a void. The mother's expression gave shape to the child's reality. The child's looking toward her for this kind of response is known as *social referencing*.

In this particular experiment, the mothers were asked to respond in one of two ways, to show either pleasure or apprehension. When the mothers looked pleased, the infants scuttled toward them, knowing that this was fun. When mother looked frightened, the baby realized the situation was dangerous and retreated.

We might suppose that at the moment when the baby glanced toward the mother's face, his or her feelings were amorphous and mixed, including both apprehension and curiosity. The mother's response is selective, determined at least in part by her own personality and experience. If a situation similar to the visual cliff arose in ordinary life, some mothers would signal anxiety and others would encourage daring. There is, however, a third possibility. The mother makes no response at all. What will be the effect? First, we presume, the child will wait, however briefly, for the mother to play her part in the child's experience. She is required, as it were, to *complete* it. If she continues to show no response, the experience has about it a feeling of being unfinished. Moreover, the child is now of two minds. Is this situation dangerous or merely interesting? What is its meaning? What reality is he or she in?

This experiment suggests that when the other fails to make adequate responses to the experiences of the child, the child will be left with a diminished sense of the reality and meaning of his or her existence. This deficit is sometimes the central presenting feature in those who have suffered a disruption in the evolution of self. One man, for example, described a lifelong feeling of unreality. This depersonalization was described in a number of ways. He felt he was living in a movie, or in a dream, or like a Martian. Even his own thoughts were strange and puzzling to him. He felt disconnected from others, often finding it difficult to follow conversations. There was, however, one situation in which he felt "solid," to use his own word. His sexual life, for a moment, made him feel real. It was as if his private world of wishes and fantasies found an answer in their enactment in the outer world. In this way, his action functioned as a mirror.

The puzzling disconnectedness and alienation of this man is illustrated in the following conversation with another patient, a professional woman, whose predicament resembles his. The woman is talking to her therapist about the fact that she can play the role given to her by her profession, but outside of it she feels unease. As she talks about this, the therapist becomes enmeshed in the patient's confusion.

> **Patient:** It goes back to when I said to you that I felt that there was something missing and I couldn't work out what.
>
> **Therapist:** What's it like to feel that something's missing?
>
> **Patient:** Well, it's like dreaming I guess.
>
> **Therapist:** Like dreaming.

Patient: Yeah.

Therapist: Well . . . it sounds like you're not even sure you can trust your own feelings.

Patient: I don't know about that.

Therapist: Do you have any reason to feel it's not real?

Patient: I know the feelings are real, what I'm asking . . . I mean they're only real because that's . . . they're only real because . . . How do you know that they're real when I haven't got another way to explain? That's the only way that I can put it into words—but how can you say that that's real? . . . Confused?

Therapist: Well, a little bit. Well, okay . . . that it's your experience of how you feel.

Patient: Yes, but . . .

Therapist: It's a little bit like you're saying "Can I tell you whether you do feel like that or not?"

Patient: How can you answer that?

Therapist: Well, can we go back to your confusion about it?

Patient: Like what?

Therapist: So, it feels like something's missing—it's like being in a dream—but you're not sure whether there is something missing and whether that's true.

Patient: Yes, that's right. And the only way that you'd say that it's real is because of a description that's put to it.

As far as is possible for her, the woman understands that reality depends upon the description that has been put to it. "What is missing" seems to be this description. The therapist comes to feel that he is required to fill the gap, knowing also that the only reality that is worthwhile is her own, not his. They are caught. She remains in a state "like dreaming."

Stories of her current experience, which she occasionally told, had a surreal quality, an eerie fragility of meaning, originating from earlier experience in which the social environment provided no mirroring responses to help reveal the nature of her personal reality.

Most children, however, have people around them who respond in a way that shows an understanding of the child's immediate and personal experience. They do so selectively. The child's developing reality is not a constant potential. It is not objectively there, to be acquired passively. Its emergence depends upon another. There is no single correct response, no true reality. Who is to say that the experience of the baby in staring down through a glass floor into a space is frightening or merely interesting? There is a range of responses from which to choose. The choice is influenced by the personality and experience of the other. The selectivity of the parent's response is evident very early in the child's life.

Very soon after birth, parents begin to give attributes to their children that often come from their own personal world and that reveal fantasies of what they hope the baby will become. The fantasies may be based on their own unfulfilled wishes. For example, in one of our studies (Meares et al. 1982), a dancing teacher with almond-shape eyes searched her child's face when she first saw her and found the same eyes. Two days later she said: "My husband keeps saying she's going to be a little ballerina. I said only if she wants to be. I mean obviously she'll come to class with me" (p. 84).

This mother is especially likely to value those aspects of the child's behavior that are consistent with her imaginative wish about who her child will become. This fantasy becomes the framework into which a life moves, constantly being shaped. This is normal. Normality is breached where the selectivity of the other acknowledges something that is not part of, or perhaps not affectively central to, the experience of the developing child. What is essential in adequate mirroring is the portrayal of what one already knows. This is beautifully described by Virginia Woolf (1925), who writes of Sir John Paston, a landowner, living in medieval England:

> Sometimes, instead of riding off on his horse to inspect his crops or bargain with his tenants, Sir John would sit, in broad daylight, reading. There, on the hard chair in the comfortless room with the wind lifting the carpet and the smoke stinging his eyes, he would sit reading Chaucer, wasting his time, dreaming—or what strange intoxication was it he drew from books? Life was rough, cheerless, and disappointing. A whole year of days would pass fruitlessly in dreary business, like dashes of rain on the window-pane. There was no reason in it as there had been for his father; no imperative need to establish a family and acquire an important position for children who were not born. . . . But Lydgate's poems or Chau-

cer's, like a mirror in which figures move brightly, silently and compactly, showed him the very skies, fields and people who he knew, but rounded and complete. Instead of waiting listlessly for news from London or piecing out from his mother's gossip some country tragedy of love and jealousy, here, in a few pages the whole story was laid before him. [pp. 23–24]

These words express the effect of language that offers no explanation of mental states, but does more than merely clarify them. Rather, an inner world is illuminated and shaped. Chaucer shows Sir John the world he knows, but more brightly, rounded and complete.

The portrayal of one's experience, which gives it reality and shape, does not always come from the faces and words of another. Sooner or later the child begins to do it for him- or herself. Although the child of 1, 2, and 3 is constantly engaged in social referencing and in seeking the mirroring responses of caregivers, there comes a time, as we have seen, when the child seems totally absorbed in play, apparently oblivious of others. At this time, his or her peculiar language has no communicative purpose. I suggest that at least one of its functions, and perhaps a principal function, is to help, together with material objects, to represent the child's embryonically inner but as yet merely personal universe. Put another way, the child is moving toward the doubling of self, taking on for him- or herself, at least for a moment, the representing function of the other.

During play, the parent, sibling, or other caregiver contributes in a way that is consistent with the play going on and that fosters it. He or she shares appropriate delight and admiration, uttering exclamations such as "Wow, look at that." He or she helps the play along by adding to the picturing of the experience, making remarks such as "that's a high one" or "he must be cross."

We come now to the clinical situation. The social environment of those with severe personality disorder has not provided mirroring of sufficient adequacy to allow the emergence of satisfactory play. In following a developmental model, the therapist tries to respond in a way that resembles mirroring but is not a replica of it. In the beginning, with very damaged patients, the imitative function is prominent. The therapist can sometimes do little more than repeat what has just been said to him or her, as in

Kohut's example (Chapter 6). Anything more promotes a disjunction. A principal difficulty, however, of responding to what is
given is that it may be part of a system of entrapment in which the
affect revealed is merely habitual, whether it be pleasant, com-
plaining, angry, or contemptuous. What is most important is to
give value and to enhance, but not steal or contaminate, that
which is spontaneous. An example, which is not common, is the
presentation of a dream. Hobson (1985) gives a beautiful example
of a mirroring response in such a circumstance.

He had been referred an aggressive, delinquent 14-year-old
boy, who, session after session, sat rigidly in his chair and
glowered at the therapist—a picture of dumb insolence. The
therapist, however, eventually made contact by talking about
cricket in an emotional way, full of the excitement of the game.
Some weeks later the boy brought a dream: "I was by a dark pool.
It was filthy and there were all sorts of horrible monsters in it. I
was scared, but I dived in and at the bottom was a great big oyster
and in it a terrific pearl. I got it and swam up again."

Hobson's reply mirrored the boy's wonder and gave value to
the experience. "That's good. Brave, too. You've got it, though,
and pearls are pretty valuable." He said nothing more. He did not
try to be a clever therapist although quite aware that the monsters
might represent sexual and aggressive wishes and of the symbolic
significance of the Pearl of Great Price. Nevertheless, in the
following sessions the boy began to talk about his life, feelings,
and frightening fantasies. He improved greatly and oriented in a
new way toward his social milieu. Only once again, many months
later, did the boy refer to the dream: "It's queer about the pearl,"
he said. "I suppose it's me in a sort of way."

Hobson's response was affectively positive and at the same
time fitted in with what was central to the boy's experience. He
did not break it up with questions or interpretations that came
from his own theoretical system.

Finally, mirroring has its dangers. The first has already been
alluded to. In responding merely to what is presented, the
therapist may be perpetuating a system of compliance. Rather
than the facade, what must be appreciated is often shown as if in
disguise, since positive emotions or creative expression had been
met in the past with responses that seemed crushing. Because of

this, the individual mentions something that is intensely charged with personal meaning, nonchalantly, matter of factly, or as if in passing. For example, a man mentioned that he was taking up painting. His first picture was of the house where he had grown up. He mentioned the subject so casually that the therapist failed to respond to it. The man dropped out of treatment a few weeks later. In contrast, a man hidden in a masklike false self system began to emerge remarkably as a consequence of murmured encouragement of the kind: "That sounds important."

A second danger of mirroring, which consists of affirmation, is that the therapist may consider it a fundamental therapeutic activity. It is not. It must always be secondary to an understanding of the most personal and immediate experience of the other. An example of this kind of mistake is provided by a therapist who mirrored the strength of a man who had resisted a suicidal impulse. The therapist, however, failed to explore and understand the individual's despair.

The therapist who believes that his or her positive and even admiring demeanor is a primary force in the generation of self risks behaving, at least at times, in a manner that is fake. Furthermore, this kind of therapist may potentiate the impediment to development of someone who is unable to enter, metaphorically, the zone of play. The therapist may respond to a series of affects in a quasi-imitative manner so that an immature face-to-face encounter goes on repetitively. Affect does not become linked to image, memory, or idea. The situation is analogous to that in which the mother replaces the transitional object and no third element emerges out of which self can grow. These two are locked in a cage of mirrors.

To conclude, mirroring is part of normal parental behavior, of which those with disorders of self have been relatively deprived. It includes parental responses that echo the pride, delight, and happiness of the child. The response shows the child what he or she feels. The representing function of mirroring gives to the child's experience meaning and reality—a kind of solidity. In ordinary mirroring, the parent responds directly to what he or she sees and hears. In the clinical situation, it is much more difficult. That which the patient values is often hidden; what must be represented is conveyed obliquely, partially, and may not be fully in the patient's awareness. The scene of play is no longer visible.

In order to make adequate responses, the therapist depends upon a capacity to imaginatively grasp those aspects of the other's experience that are not in view. We come now to the subject of empathy.

EMPATHY AND
Chapter 16 | # DECENTRATION

The therapist's capacity for empathy is the principal agent for change in his or her patient. Why should this be so? To answer this question, we return to the metaphor of the play space. At play, the child is often telling a story. This is not true merely for middle-class children of the West. Lois Barclay Murphy (1972) was astonished to discover, in a study in India, that children in this very different culture played in the same way as did American children.

In play, children project the "basic time-space patterns of their lives" (Murphy, p. 119). This seems to have been the case for many thousands of years. Artifacts from the earliest civilizations include miniature representations of people and animals, presumably used as toys. It is difficult not to conclude that the capacity to play is part of our genetic endowment, just as a potential for language creation is biologically given.[1] Unlike, say, the ability to walk, this capacity depends upon the responsiveness of the environment. Murphy found that children from deprived, poverty-ridden backgrounds were often unable to play with materials in a way that revealed a theme. Although these children could indulge in sensory play with sand, water, clay and finger paints – and to wash a baby doll or make a sand pie, they did not project sequences of experience and behavior. This kind of play depends upon caregivers responding so as to facilitate it. They show some understanding of and sensitivity to what is being expressed in play. The understanding involves imagination. For example, a little girl of 4, whose mother and two aunts are all pregnant, places a kitchen stove, a toilet, and a baby in a crib. Does this express the fear that when all these babies arrive there will be no care left over for the child, so that she will have to have her own things? Or does it betray her puzzlement about how the babies, squashed inside their mothers' abdomens, manage for food and elimination? The mother's participation in the story, which does not take it over, follows her imaginative understanding. In this way, she helps the story move on and develop. To some extent, she is being empathic. However, empathy of the kind that the clinical situation demands is more complex.

Kohut defined empathy as *vicarious introspection*. The patient begins to describe an experience and the therapist tries to follow him or her in an imaginative way into this region. I have visualized their joint activity in terms of a metaphoric screen.[2] The patient's expressed thought processes are, as it were, projected and placed before the eyes rather as one watches the projection of images at a movie. It is, however, a curious film, since it is being made as it is watched. As the patient throws upon the screen glimpses of half-seen forms, faint outlines, the therapist tries to fill in the gaps and make out the shapes.

This description is of an ideal and not particularly common situation. Nevertheless, it represents that toward which the therapist strives. The therapist's task, together with that of the patient, is for insight into the patient's world – insight being used in its original sense – seeing with the eye of the mind, having inner vision (Oxford English Dictionary). Being empathic with an adult means listening and perceiving in a certain way so as to grasp some aspects of his or her inner experience. With a child at play, however, personal experience is not yet inner. It is displayed for the caregiver to view. Vicarious introspection is not needed. The caregiver is an *actual* spectator upon the psychic life of the child. This scene, however, provides a model for conceiving the empathic stance. The metaphor of the view of, or perspective upon, the psychic life of another is central to it. The therapist is required to behave rather like the sensitive caregiver at the scene of play, fostering the activity in which a personal reality, or self, is being generated and represented.

The duality of the empathic stance is suggested in the model of play. The adult participant is both spectator of and also, in some imaginative way, *in* the play. I approach this essential duality from several directions, the first being historical.

Perhaps the earliest description of empathy, at least in the modern age, came from Desiderius Erasmus. In his *Praise of Folly* (1511), he argued that "the whole man" had the capacity for a curious state of mind, which he likened to madness or folly, although not quite seriously. He also likened this state to love: "He who loves intensely no longer lives in himself but in whatever he loves, and the more he can depart from himself and enter into the other, the happier he is. And when a mind yearns toward travelling out of the body, and does not rightly use its own bodily organs, you doubtless, and with accuracy, call the state of it madness" (p. 123). This notion seems central to the Erasmian philosophy but is also fundamental to an understanding of empathy. What is most important, in the state that Erasmus described, is that one imaginatively inhabits the other person, at the same time retaining one's own "soul." Michael Screech (1988) points out that his idea was revolutionary in that it reversed the teaching of St. Paul. The Pauline assertion was "I live, yet not I but Christ liveth in me" (Screech, p. 151), whereas Erasmus suggests that the highest form of experiencing involves the capacity to "migrate" into another. For St. Paul the movement was in the opposite direction, so that he was inhabited by Christ. Erasmus implies that this is a relatively low form of rapture, found, for example, in the pseudo-Dionysians. Put another way, it is the basis of cult formation. It is also one of the forms of sympathy,[3] a subject to which we return later.

The next major exploration of empathy came from the Neapolitan philosopher, Giovanni Battista Vico (1668–1744). His ideas were novel, beyond the understanding of his own age, so that they had little influence in his day and were virtually forgotten after his death until a century later. In 1724 he finished a treatise in which he refuted the views of rationalists like Descartes and

Spinoza, and utilitarians such as Locke and Hobbes. Since these men were the most admired thinkers of their time, Vico's patron refused to fund the publication of the treatise. Vico eventually cut the book to a quarter of its size, including only his own positive ideas. This book *The New Science* was his masterpiece.

The starting point of Vico's ideas was the conviction that the methods of Descartes could not usefully be applied outside the fields of mathematics and the natural sciences. Disciplines such as psychology, history, and anthropology could not be approached simply by measurement and logic. As Berlin (1977) put it: "Whatever the splendours of the exact sciences there was a sense in which we could know more about our own and other men's experiences—in which we acted as participants, indeed authors, and not as mere observers—than we could ever know about non-human nature which we could only observe from outside" (p. 12). This knowledge was gained by entering into the minds of others by means of *fantasia*—"man's unique capacity for imaginative insight and reconstruction" (p. 108). We know little about another culture or period of history if our only information is a chronicle of events or a catalog of artifacts. We need, in addition, to know something of the mind of that society. How else, for example, could the rituals of an African or native American society be understood?

A German, Johann Gottfried Herder (1744–1803), was perhaps the next major advocate for empathy. He added to the concept of Vico by emphasizing the role of feeling. He introduced the term *Einfuhlen*, maintaining that the scholar of any civilization is required to "feel himself" into the essence of its life.

It is customary to suppose that the concept of empathy was introduced into Anglo-American thinking through the concept of *einfuhlen*, as described by Dilthey and Lipps (Lichtenberg et al. 1984) who were writing a century after Herder. However, the American, Charles Cooley (1902), described something similar at about the same time. He used the term *sympathetic imagination* to describe our capacity to look at things as others in different situations do and have the feelings others have in circumstances actually different from our own. Nevertheless, until quite recently, empathy has not fared well in the Anglo-American world. It appears only in a supplement of the *Oxford English Dictionary*. It was not included in *Webster's Dictionary* until quite recently. It is sometimes considered to be merely a synonym for sympathy. In order to show the difference between these two phenomena, we now turn to a brief consideration of sympathy.

Something like sympathy can be observed very early in life. Soon after birth, babies in a nursery with other newborns cry when another infant cries.[4] This is the earliest evidence of sympathy. It might be seen as something like contagion—one of the features of the definition of sympathy. We might speculate, however, that the baby's actual experience is of someone crying within him or her, as if the baby who is crying and the baby whose crying has been triggered commingle. It might be that the baby senses in some primitive and unformed way the crying within him or her as a signal of distress and cries in response.

As adults we may also see the baby's crying in response to another's cry as evidence of compassion. This would probably be an error of the kind Kohut has called adultomorphic. Nevertheless, it does appear that as sympathy develops, it seems to be based on something like a fellow feeling. Martin Hoffman (1978), for example, gave a description of a boy about 18 months old who when distressed would suck his thumb and pull his ear. One day, the little boy was upset when he became aware that his father was distressed. He went up to his father and began to pull his father's ear lobe at the same time sucking his own thumb. Again, there is a commingling of the individual and the other for whom compassion is felt. In this case, however, there has been a progression. Whereas the newborn child was inhabited by the cries of another or the experience of another, in the case of the 18-month-old, the reverse seems to be happening. There are elements of identification in this story. The little boy has put himself in the place of his father and for a moment becomes him. When the child conceives more completely of the distinction between himself and those close to him, a more mature form of identification occurs—the individual puts him- or herself in the place of the other and experiences those things that he or she would feel in such a situation. This, however, is not yet empathy, since at this stage the identification does not involve feeling as the *other* would feel.

Certain essentials of empathy can be derived from such disparate sources as those anecdotes of children's behavior, the model of play, and the history of the concept of empathy. From the model of play we gain the notion of perspective, the idea that empathy involves something like a view upon the experience of another. From Vico we are given the idea of a different kind of thought process being involved, that of fantasia. From Herder and his notion of *Einfuhlen*, we gain the essential ingredient of feeling — we cannot truly know the experience of another unless somehow or other we feel the emotion that is at the core of it. Finally, from the children's studies we become aware that the identification involved in empathy is a curious one because it is not precisely oneself who is placed within the experience of the other. What is required is a strange kind of identification in which, as far as possible, one's own personal world of feelings, prejudices, wishes, and so on is removed. In this way, to return to Flavell's study of children's gift giving, the boy of 6 is able to abandon the belief that his mother might be especially excited to receive a toy truck as a present and realize that nylon stockings might be preferred. Empathy then requires a kind of identification that is impersonal. At the same time it demands a perspective upon that identification. The individual, in Piagetian terms, moves from the egocentric phase of early childhood to a position that is decentered, from which it can be appreciated that others have worlds that are quite different to one's own.[5] In my view, this cannot emerge until there is a sense of one's own world, which is conceived as distinct to that of others. Following this idea, we find that those with disorders of self are often deficient in the area of empathy. As a consequence, others frequently regard them as exploitative.

We come now to the clinical implications of an empathic stance. It is clear that the therapist's contributions based on empathy are different from those that involve a personal identification, which is the basis of sympathy. Sympathy is of very little value and, indeed, can be seen as contributing to a system of entrapment. Empathy, in contrast, offers the means of escape. Sympathy, which involves something like compassion, might provoke a remark such as "How terrible." The same story told to someone acting empathically might produce a remark such as "You felt like killing him." It seems clear that one difference between sympathy and empathy is that the former does not depend upon an imaginative awareness of the state of the other. Consequently, it does not promote its growth.

It is essential in using the empathic approach that the therapist recognizes that it is not his or her task to be clever and to accurately tell the patient what he or she is thinking or feeling. The task is to bring into being a state like play, which must depend upon an understanding of experiences that are going on inside the patient. The therapist is not required to be an oracle or a seer, but a facilitator. The patient's material should not be used to display the therapist's brilliance, but rather as means of amplification of the patient's own awareness. The sense that the experiences are the patient's own must not be tampered with. The interpretations of the therapist should not steal or contaminate the experience by, for example, explanations and decoding. An empathic approach can be illustrated in the response to dreams.

Dream material is of value since it is personal and not produced by mere stimuli. The therapist, highly trained in the subject of symbolic representation, may be tempted to tell the patient about the patient's own dream. In my view, this is not a suitable approach. Rather, the therapist, who may have a very good idea of the significance of the dream, should behave in a manner that allows the patient to explore the dream for him- or herself. He or she should initially respond, not to the content of the dream and its meaning, but to some quality of the dream, in the manner of mirroring. A comment may be made, for example, on the creativeness, the beauty, the sadness, the strangeness of the dream. For example, a woman of about 40 who leads a life virtually without relationships and who seems unable to talk of personal matters beyond the day to day, recounts her dream in which her mother takes her car and damages it. The therapist, although well aware that the car may be a representation of self, remarks simply that it is a strong dream. In an unobtrusive way the therapist keeps the car in focus and the two of them seem to wander around the subject. The patient wonders whether to get a new car, tells of her mother's exhortations that she drive carefully, and so on. Then the patient says, "I'm fond of the car. Any change in the engine noise while I'm driving and I get a little palpitation. I feel it is a threat to my safety." In the end, the patient makes her own connection between herself and her car. This is of far more value than the therapist having made it for her and, in this way, stolen her discovery. What is required now is some validation, some affirming response on the part of the therapist. What the therapist says is "right" in a very encouraging tone. The therapist then asks, "Can you tell me more about that?" She also might have said a number of things that may have been effective. She might have said, for example, "As if there's something of you in the car."

The therapist's response, however, is a good one because it allows the patient to move on. The patient says, "My car allows me to get from A to B without my relying on anyone else." This seems to imply that the car is a means of gaining some autonomy, perhaps some sense of agency in a world in which the mother seems the only agent. The therapist says, "So it is very important. To think of the car being ruined is very frightening." In this case, the empathy of the therapist has failed. The patient simply replies, "Yeah," and there is a long pause. The theme is lost. The exploration is stopped. The therapist's response has not been near enough to the patient's experience to allow its further unraveling.

The therapist's role in empathically engaging with the patient has similarities to what Bruner (1983) had called *scaffolding*. While the child plays with objects, the mother helps. However, she does not do this by playing with the objects herself. Rather she arranges things, so that the child is better able to achieve a construction to which he or she seems to be striving. The therapist's contribution and the mother's activity both help the process to move on. Something happens that could not have happened without this social environment.

The next point to consider in the clinical application of empathy is language. The grammatical structure of the language influences the emergence of the empathic engagement. Where the grammatical structure is impersonal, it is enhanced. The therapist tends to use few pronouns, making remarks that might be metaphorically perceived as directed toward the play space or some invisible cinematic screen. "It looks like . . ." "It seems there is something else . . ." As previously noted, the use of language in which pronouns are emphasized promotes a relationship between subject and object rather than between subject and selfobject.

A second quality of the language of empathy is that it fits in with the language of play, or inner speech as Vygotsky called it. The therapist's remarks tend to be associative, laden with feeling and abbreviated. They should not break up the metaphoric play.

A third element, which can be touched on here only briefly,

concerns the use of metaphor. Since ultimately the aim is to develop the interior life and to foster the feelings and imaginings that are peculiarly personal to a particular individual, one requires a language that will somehow describe this inner life. However, the intangible movements of inner life can only be conveyed by means of things that can be seen and touched (Meares 1985). Emotions, at the bottom, are always expressed in terms of metaphor. Words for affect are dead metaphors. For example, sadness originally meant heaviness; joy meant brightness. The therapist needs to be sensitively aware of metaphors that do not have the extravagance of literary productions, but are unobtrusively hidden in the patient's expression. They may be the means of helping to enlarge and make real something of the inner zone.

Finally, we come to the effect of what is essential to the empathic stance—decentration. The empathic stance offers a way beyond entrapment and a life lived at the mercy of stimuli. A curious paradox now becomes evident—the individual can only discover his or her own center by being able to move outside it. This process is fostered when the therapist with whom the individual feels connected is constantly engaged in attempting to establish a duality that is central to empathy. The therapist, while maintaining the connectedness with the patient, is constantly moving the patient's awareness toward those fleeting glimpses of that which is inner. In terms of the basic metaphor, the therapist is trying to move the patient's experience from a world that is real to a world that resembles the playroom. The therapist's discipline in maintaining, as far as possible, a perspective upon the experience in which both partners are immersed encourages a movement toward the patient's being able to grasp the spatiality of his or her existence.

Finally, it is interesting to return to Erasmus, since he seemed to be saying that the state of mind we now call empathy enables one to go beyond the entrapment of stimuli, and indeed this is its purpose. He wrote (1511): "The great masses of people admire what things are most corporeal and deem that such come near to being the only things they are. The religious, on the contrary, pay less attention to anything the more nearly it concerns the body, and they are wholly rapt away in the contemplation of things unseen" (p. 120).

Chapter 17 | ERROR AND THE TRANSFERENCE

Empathy inevitably fails. Nobody can know, completely, the more personal and intimate aspects of the reality of another. In many cases the empathic failure is quite useful. It confirms for the patient that his or her inner life is not totally accessible to others. Put another way, the failure has a value because it affirms the distinction between an inner world and the outer one.

The second way in which the failure is beneficial is related. The patient comes to realize that the therapist is not omniscient and omnipotent. This discovery is something like that of the 4-year-old Edmund Gosse when his father failed to know of the boy's misdemeanor. Kohut (1984), who more than any other therapist has emphasized the value of therapeutic failure, made an analogy between the effect of the undetected lie and empathic failure. He wrote: "The place of the undetected lie is rather taken by the analyst and discovery that his own understanding of his mental states and attitudes is better at times than that of the analyst, that the analyst is not omniscient, that is empathy is fallible, and that the patient's empathy with himself, including, par excellence, his empathy with his childhood experiences, is often superior" (p. 72).

Kohut's idea parallels that of Winnicott, who considered, as noted in previous chapters, that it was necessary for the child to go through a period of omnipotence. This must be related to a conception of the other as omniscient. It is necessary, as Winnicott pointed out, that following this phase, the child, in small doses, is exposed to disillusion. In this way, slowly the child begins to learn that there is a world that is different from his own and that might be called the real world. Indeed, toward the end of his life, Winnicott remarked that the purpose of his interpretations was to show the limits of his understanding.

Not only is it important for the patient to know that the therapist is not fully able to comprehend his or her inner world, it is often extraordinarily helpful for the therapist to acknowledge that he was incorrect. He need only say something simple like "That wasn't quite right, was it?" for something profound to occur within the patient. The reasons are several. First, nobody may have said such a thing before. Second, it is possible that the therapist, in making this remark, immediately establishes a reconnection with the patient through showing that he has actually understood what had happened at that moment, that although he had failed just before, the bond between them has not been lost. There is a sense of relief.

Those with disorders of self are extraordinarily sensitive to disjunctions, as we have seen. Furthermore, these disjunctions have an effect that is beyond anything that could be anticipated in a person whose development has been relatively unimpeded. A remark such as "I don't think I quite understand" may provoke profound despair. One of Kohut's most important contributions was to show that this experience, on the face of it deleterious, can be very valuable if approached in the right way. It is important that the experience be explored, first of all, at the point of immediacy, where the disjunction occurred.

The above incident implies that the mistake of the therapist is not necessarily a large one. *Optimal frustration*, as Kohut termed it, is required.[1] In writing on the subject, Kohut seemed to identify two main forms of optimal frustration. In the first case, it is nonspecific, of the kind described so far. The second form, however, is more particularly related to the personal system of the patient. In this sense it is specific. The error may not be an error in any technical sense. Nevertheless, it repeats a trauma from the patient's past. This phenomenon leads us to the concept of transference. Transference is the experiencing of someone in the present as if he were a figure in the past. This is the centerpiece of psychoanalysis of the classical kind. In the model I describe, it is also central. However, the way in which it is approached is different. In this system, the model of transference is based on a therapeutic error of the specific kind. Transference is considered an impediment to play.

Kohut (1984) described the origin of the effect of the therapeutic error in the following way. "The patient self-disintegrates temporarily because the withdrawal of the mirroring selfobject repeats the traumatic unavailability of self confirming responses in early life" (p. 102). This incident reflects "a transference experience that is due to a revived development need" (p. 102). An example of this kind of error is found in Chapter 9. The therapist, by remaining silent, failed to provide the requisite mirroring atmosphere just as the patient's mother had failed. In this case, a threat to the integrity of self arises through a selfobject failure of a very minor kind, which repeats a much earlier and traumatic failure. The disjunction precipitates the transference phenomena. It also breaks up any potential for the kind of mental activity that underlies symbolic play and in which a sense of self can be generated. To repeat, transference is an impediment to play. This idea is illustrated in the following summary of a session.

THE SESSION

The patient, a policeman who had been referred for treatment of frightening fits of violence, had been in therapy for about a year. There has been considerable progress and fears were no longer held for the safety of his family. Nevertheless, the therapist has suggested that it may be desirable to maintain the frequency of sessions. The patient seemed reluctant.

The session begins with the patient's complaints about the heavy rain he had had to travel through on the way to the session.

Therapist: How did you feel about coming today?

Patient: I don't really know how I felt (pause). Sort of funny really, my trail bike has been sitting there. It's been a real mix-up with the parts that I need for it. I told you about the bike shop?

[The therapist's inquiry has triggered a disjunction, although the therapist is not aware of it, since there is very little change of affect as conveyed in the patient's tone of voice. The content, however, betrays what has happened. The patient's discourse is linear and outer-directed. There is now a long description of the difficulties in procuring parts. However, a new element is soon introduced. It concerns pressure. It seems that it's a hassle to get to the Yamaha shop. The patient says: "See, that's something I've been putting off. Although it's at my own convenience, I still put it off because a simple thing like that makes me feel pressured." The therapist attempts a suggestion that connects pressure with the patient's having to come to the session, but he cannot finish it. The patient talks over him. The therapist does not persist. After further talk of hassles, the therapist continues.]

Therapist: So you end up feeling scared off by all the hassles.

Patient: Yeah, no such thing as simple parts service anymore.

Therapist: I guess that makes you feel pretty vulnerable, being in that situation.

[The therapist's remarks are unexpected. There has been nothing to suggest anxiety or vulnerability in the patient's story of his hassles. Yet they have a positive effect. The patient begins to talk of his wife, for whom "nothing's a hassle" and soon reveals that "it was sort of pressuring me coming" that is, to the sessions.]

Therapist: It was almost getting to the point where I was telling you to come, like maybe your father might . . .

Patient: Ah, in a way I felt a bit pressured like when I knew you didn't want to cut down the sessions.

The patient goes on to describe the pushiness of his father. The session has now been going 12 minutes. What has transpired involves a form of transference: as Freud (1905) indicates, "a whole series of psychological experiences are revived, not as belonging to the past, but as applying to the person of the physician at the present moment" (p. 116). The therapist is perceived as pressuring the patient, just as his father did. This brief episode also illustrates a contemporary view of transference, which emphasizes that the experience of the patient is not only determined by the past but also by the present. As Gill (1985) puts it: "The emphasis shifts from looking upon the transference as determined solely by the patient in essential disregard of the current therapeutic situation to understanding how, at the very least, the transference has been stimulated by or is a response to the therapist" (p. 90). This view changes transference from being a single-person phenomenon to one in which the interaction between two people is involved. Furthermore, it is not simply the past that appears in this interaction but also the present. This is apparent in the illustrative session. The patient's experience comes not only from the past but also the present. The therapist, *in fact*, put pressure on the patient by apparently focusing, in his query that opened the session, on the patient's presumed reluctance. In this case at least, the form of the disjunction mirrors the form of the transference.

If the task of the therapist were to show the distortions of his patient's perception of him, that is, to offer him insight, the therapist's work would have been completed, at least for this episode. This, however, is not the primary aim. Rather, the main objective is to repair the disjunction in order to restart a form of mental functioning during which growth can occur. This would have been easier had the therapist realized the effect of his opening remark. However, his constant attempt to understand his patient and to express some of his understanding ultimately has its effect. The beginning of the repair of the disjunction begins when the therapist makes his speculation about the patient's anxiety and vulnerability. His understanding arises from previous sessions. The reparative process continues during the next minute as the patient elaborates on his father's pushiness.

> **Patient:** So, do you get what I mean?
>
> **Therapist:** Yeah, sounds a bit like you end up being ignored.
>
> **Patient:** Um, well, yeah. You ask for something, he'll agree to help more or less only in the way that he thinks you should be helped, not in what you're actually asking. You don't want what he tells you you should want. So from that he can get very pushy.
>
> **Therapist:** Was that the way you thought I was being?
>
> **Patient:** In a way yeah . . . it's a similarity. I can't quite pinpoint it.
>
> **Therapist:** Mm, hmm.

Patient: If you said like "Yeah, I agree, it should be what you want, but I really think you should come twice a week regardless," well that's the sort of pushiness, that would be the similarity. . . .

Therapist: Yeah.

Patient: Getting off the track, I really enjoyed it though . . . I quite like it sometimes.

[At this point something remarkable happens. The patient's words seem to have no connection with the conversation. "Getting off the track" comes out of the blue and represents the ending of the sense of disjunction. In terms of metaphor, the patient has, for a moment, entered the play space. This change in the mode of being with the other has been triggered, or facilitated, by the therapist's continuing efforts to establish the requisite enabling atmosphere. The switch, however, of the patient's experiential mode is too fast for the therapist to track. He does not notice it. Nevertheless, this failure does not cause the patient to leave an imaginative zone entirely. He begins reflecting back, in his words, on his early adult life, finding in it positive aspects he had not seen before. He reflects also upon experiences, such as travel, that he's missed out on. The word *regret* comes up, mirroring the tone of his voice. After about 7 minutes, the therapist makes a response that tries to put into words the sense of regret. This triggers a reply, which makes clear what is meant by "getting off the track."]

Patient: And the more I think about trying to find what it is I want to do . . . I'd like to get on my bike and just drift for a couple of months. Just give my notice and just hop on my bike, go south or west, for a couple of months, live in a caravan.

Therapist: Yeah.

Patient: I think it'd be great to go and just do that, just drift around for a while. It'd be pretty lonely I suppose, 'cause it's not like I'm known in the west. I'd just like to go somewhere different, just drift, enjoy my bike. That's something I can't do, as long as you've got a wife and family and house.

[Once more, the patient kicks into a different mode of experiencing. He conjures up a sense of flow, a drift through relatively empty, pure space. It is tempting to suppose that the wandering is a metaphor for play, that the continent is the play space, and that the bike has transitional qualities, in the Winnicottian sense. This is supported by the clinical history. The only person the patient remembers as giving him care when he was a child was his grandfather. He felt content being with his grandfather while the old man tinkered with machines, such as his motorcycle. This biographical information helps to further our understanding of the session's opening, when following the disjunction, the patient begins to talk, in a way that seems trivial and irrelevant, about motorcycle parts. The conversation, here, enters the zone of the secret.]

Kohut (1971, 1977) has pointed out that massive disjunctions provided by the therapist's vacation, for example, may trigger behavior such as perverse, bizarre, or compulsive sexual activity, which at first sight is entirely unadaptive. Exploration of these experiences, however, often reveals a fantasy that has an integrative effect (see Chapter 9). In the same way, smaller disjunctions that arise through the therapist's failure to understand may activate images or behavior that help to restore a threatened sense of self. Repetitive tinkering with and a preoccupation with motorcycle parts may have had the effect of "holding" this particular man when his sense of cohesiveness was momentarily disrupted.

To return to the session: The therapist's reply misses the emergence of the spontaneous material.

Therapist: Sounds like you end up feeling that this responsibility stops you from doing anything.

This remark points to the person of the patient as *you* rather than at the production of his imagination. In attempting to foster a mental activity that resembles that underlying the child's play, the therapist must, together with the patient, metaphorically gaze toward the play space. This activity can also be figuratively conceived as directed toward a screen, as if at the movie theater (Chapter 16). Since the therapist's remarks concern what is happening there, they tend to have an impersonal grammatical function.

When the therapist uses pronouns, he or she tends to turn the attention of both parties away from the exploration of the patient's interior world. The activity of the therapist ceases to be vicarious introspection. The use of pronouns, however, is appropriate to the disjunctional mode of relating in which the therapist is experienced as an object, a *you* rather than a selfobject. Grammatical organization helps to structure the form of a relationship (Havens 1978, 1979). The therapist's use of a pronoun at this point in the session helps to provoke a small disjunction.

The patient, however, is not completely thrown off course. He returns to reflecting upon his early adult life. His excursions into these memories are extensive, taking up much of the remainder of the session. The therapist tries to follow him, and slowly the story becomes more personal. The man begins to express a feeling of some fundamental lack, of having been deprived of ordinary experiences that other people had and that leaves him with a feeling of being handicapped, perhaps irredeemably. All he knows about is engines.

With this awareness of lack and deprivation comes another awareness, of a need to find a way by which to generate those core experiences that are basic to an ordinary sense of existence. This sense of need seems to be related to the fantasy of wandering with his bike through the interior of the continent.

In summary, this session illustrates the effect of disjunctions between the patient's personal reality and the therapist's understanding of it or response to its expression. The disjunction threatens this personal reality. There is a diminishment, perhaps quite slight, in the sense of self. A new state of self is precipitated (in this case, feeling pressured), which is linked to a perception of the other (pushy). At times, a memory of an experience that had been calming, which is represented symbolically (playing with motorcycle parts) may also follow the disjunction. Two persons, not one, are involved in the disjunction. The patient's experience is not simply determined by the past. It is triggered by an event in the present that often echoes the original trauma it evokes. Following the disjunction, there is a condensation of what has just happened and what is remembered. This state is an impediment, blocking access to a kind of mental activity that is necessary to growth. The therapist's task is to remove the impediment, starting with the patient's view of the actual experience.

These incidents and also those in which the patient momentarily enters the play space provide models for conceiving the significance of transference phenomena.

Before further considering this matter, it is necessary to review briefly the traditional approach so that differences between the two models can be displayed.

METAPHORS OF MIND

Metaphor necessarily underlies a theory of mind. The metaphor upon which early psychoanalysis was based was a compelling one. When Freud began to work on developing his theory of psychoanalysis, he did so in an intellectual climate that Ellenberger (1970), in his great book, has beautifully outlined. One of the principal ideas forming this climate is what Ellenberger has called the *pathogenic secret*. He traces the story of this model of psychological healing through a number of cultures. The patient is conceived as if he has within himself a bad experience that rots within him like a malignancy. It must be removed for cure to occur. In some cultures the badness is concretized as a foreign body. The shaman, at the end of the healing ritual, demonstrates to the sick person the thing that had been in his body and had been causing the illness. In other cultures the evil within is less concretized, perhaps as a spirit that has to be expelled through exorcism. In our own culture, confession has been one of the means of voidance of the secret. In Vienna, Moritz Benedict published a series of papers from 1864 to 1895 in which he suggested that neurotic illness was often caused by secrets, often pertaining to sexual life, and that cure came with their removal through catharsis. When Breuer and Freud produced *Studies in Hysteria* (1895), which Brill (1937) called the *"fons et origo* of psychoanalysis,"* they described a hidden experience, characteristically sexual, which was at the bottom of the illness. It had to be removed, in their words, "like a foreign body" (p. 7).

As psychoanalysis developed on this basis, it became intricately elaborated. The contents of the secret changed from trauma to the unacceptable wishes underlying the oedipal drama. The mechanism of hiddenness became more complex. Over the years, the system that kept hidden the unacceptable drives and wishes became increasingly emphasized. Out of this theoretical development, focusing on ego, grew a number of secondary metaphors of a hydraulic and energic kind. Despite the increasingly complex theory of drive, conflict, and defense, the task of the therapist remained the same. At bottom, his or her endeavors were directed to evading the mechanisms of defense by such means as following the implications of the form of the transference and in this way discovering what was hidden, the pathogenic secret. In terms of this model, the principal aim was insight. As Arlow (1985) put it, "The essential principle of the entire psychotherapeutic approach . . . is to demonstrate to the patient the persistent effect of the unconscious wishes that originated during childhood" (p. 117).

By the beginning of the 1970s, it had become apparent to many authorities that treatment based, at bottom, on the metaphor of the pathogenic secret was not suitable for severe personality disorder. Other modes of treatment gained increasing acceptance. Nevertheless, they were not based on any metaphor as compelling as that of the early days. Freud, however, in an almost throwaway remark, implied an alternative. He made an analogy between the transference and a play space *(spielraum)*.[2]

The metaphor of the play space, conceived in a way that is consistent with emerging ideas about the understanding of the borderline experience orients therapeutic work with transference phenomena differently than the approach described, for example, by Arlow. Rather than using transference phenomena as a means to uncovering unconscious wishes that originated in childhood, they are considered in relation to a generation of a sense of self. Following the metaphor of the play space, two contrasting forms of transference become apparent. The first of these might be called selfobject transferences; the second arise as impediments to the evolution of self.

Selfobject transferences should, perhaps, not be called transferences since, in an extreme case, they represent an experience that the patient has never had. Rather, they are manifestations of something like a drive toward a state of being with another in which those experiences that make up a core of self can be created. They represent, in the words of Ornstein, "a thwarted need to grow" (p. 47). Kohut has identified two forms of these necessary experiences of being with another. He called them *mirroring* and *idealizing*. Put another way, the damaged person has an almost intuitive realization that some fundamental lack in the sense of existence can be overcome in a relationship in which there is not only approval but also a sensitive responsiveness to one's most central personal experience. An idealization pervades this kind of relationship. It is important to note that this atmosphere of idealization is relatively nonsalient. Neither the playing child nor the patient who feels understood may be quite aware of it.

The drive to establish mirroring and idealizing transferences is repeatedly impeded by another form of transference, which is the response to a disruption in the connectedness between self and the other as selfobject. In this case, the experience of the other is salient, occupying the forefront of consciousness. The therapist is now an object. (A pathological idealization, fueled by anxiety, is not an uncommon form of this kind of transference.) The relationship is now between a *you* and an *I*. The aim of the therapeutic response is to allow this construction of him or her, which occupies the foreground of consciousness, to retreat and eventually to atrophy. This allows the other kind of transference to emerge in which the therapist is experienced as a selfobject.

Play can now begin. The therapist's contributions are now no longer directed at the two people in the room. Rather, they concern a third element that has arisen, toward which, as it were, both partners gaze. Since what is viewed is an inner world, the therapist's stance is something like vicarious introspection. The language is now more associative.[3] Distortions of perception of the therapist during the impeding transference will usually be explored. Although changes in the distortions may subsequently occur, this is not the primary therapeutic purpose. The aim is not the delivery of insight. Rather, it is to further the kind of mental activity that underpins the play of the preoperational child. Out of this emerges, it is supposed, a small change in the structuralized representation in memory of the momentary experiences of self.[4]

In conclusion, this session illustrates the main point of the book. A young man talking about motorcycle parts and his personal relationships introduces an element that is different from the rest of his story and that seems peculiarly personal, related to some imaginative idea about finding himself. For a moment he seems to enter the zone of the secret.[5] It is not something to be found and confessed in the manner of the pathogenic secret. Rather, the discovery and creative elaboration of this zone of experience, which may be unrealized or only dimly part of consciousness, is an ideal toward which work with those with disturbances of self is aimed. In a suitable environment, what was hidden now becomes part of the play space, in which can be generated a sense of self.

Chapter 18 | A DRIVE TO PLAY

R obert Hobson (1985) has written of a chimpanzee studied by Wolfgang Kohler:

> Tschego, an adult female, treasured a single stone; smooth, round and polished by the sea. She sat gazing at it, fondled it, and took it to bed with her. She would never part with it. Tschego would greet a young monkey by pressing his/her hand to her lap as she did to Kohler and some other humans.
>
> She will press our hand to just that spot between her upper thigh and lower abdomen where she keeps her precious objects. She herself, as a greeting, will put her huge hand to the other animal's lap or between their legs and she is inclined to extend this greeting even to men. [Kohler 1925, p. 99]

The stone had no obvious practical usefulness, such as for throwing at other offending monkeys or cracking nuts. It had *significance*. It was more than a signal. There was a suggestion of an "inner" reference since Tschego, when alone, behaved as if it were a precious treasure. Furthermore, it was a currency in social situations. Perhaps, here, we see something of the beginning of symbolism of a language of feeling in relationships. [Hobson 1985, pp. 82–83]

The chimpanzee used the stone much as a child uses the transitional object. This anecdote suggests that primates other than humans engage in some forms of symbolic play. Taken together with other disparate pieces of evidence, such as McLean's (1986) relating the play of animals to the cingulate gyrus, we might infer that we are born with a propensity, instinct, or drive to play.

Early psychoanalysis postulated only two drives, sex and aggression, motivating human behavior. Freud, however, found in himself another imperative. In describing his choice of career, he wrote (1925): "I was moved rather by a sort of curiosity, which was, however, directed more towards human concerns than towards natural objects" (p. 8). His curiosity was a force that shaped his life. In recent years the list of motivational forces that are generally supposed to have some neurophysiological basis has increased greatly beyond the original two. It now includes curiosity. It is seen as an aspect of a motivational system that also includes symbolic play.[1]

Our innate biological equipment includes certain impulses that push us toward those situations and activities that are required for existence and growth. Studies of attachment behavior show that this is so not only for simple physico-chemical needs such as food and water, but also for those of a psychological and interpersonal kind. Expressions of drives in these spheres are not always recognized as such. The following session provides an illustration.

> With a strange intensity and absorption, a man in his thirties tells his therapist of an Indian guru he has heard about. The guru has, it appears, supernatural powers, and as a consequence has amassed great wealth. Nevertheless, he has, in the view of the patient, been neither exploitative nor manipulative. He has done "good things" with his money. It is clear that the image of the guru is idealized. Moreover, it is connected with the therapist who is seen as an expert on theology, about which the patient asks questions. However, he seems to expect no answer. When the therapist responds, a different kind of monologue is triggered. The atmosphere of idealization vanishes. It concerns the mass of people who are aggressive and jealous, who bump him on the bus,

who allow him no space of his own, and for whose arrogance he feels contempt. These digressions are brief, and the patient soon returns to the main theme. This changes to a description of an essential lack. It concerns his education. Since he left school early, he feels that he is irretrievably deficient and that nothing can redeem what he has not been given. Interestingly, he thinks about overcoming it, not by entering night school or applying for mature age education, but by writing. He has made numerous inquiries about courses of instruction that might somehow allow him to know how and what to write. As the session ends, the man makes the point of his preoccupations clear. He asks the therapist how he can find a life with meaning for himself.

This man's meandering talk concerning the guru and the possibility of writing is not mere chatter. His absorption in what he says shows its importance. The story of the young man with the motorcycle in the previous chapter helps us to identify the underlying ideas and feelings. Like the man with the motorcycle, this man senses within himself a fundamental lack. He has an ill-defined intuition that in order to overcome it, he needs to find an idealized figure who will not harm him. In the same way that we know we need food, water, and air, he seems to know the conditions necessary to growth in the psychic sphere.

In this session, the therapist is experienced as a potential selfobject. However, every time she speaks, she breaks the developing atmosphere. Her remarks are factual, too concerned with the guru and not enough concerned with the skein of feelings, wishes, and imaginings that underlie the patient's words. The therapist now becomes an object and an impediment to the individual's drive toward health, as described in the previous chapter. The sense of impediment evokes momentary anger, perceptible in the content but not the tone of the conversation. The therapist becomes, briefly, one of those who, metaphorically, bump into the patient, allowing him no space to grow. These manifestations of transference, however, are brief. He returns to the feeling that he has missed something essential in his development. Whereas the man with the motorcycle concretized this lack in terms of travel, this patient conceived the deficiency in terms of education. In each case, what is lacking is a sense of self. Each man has his own solution. For one, it is wandering; for the other, it is writing. Both activities can be seen as analogs of play. Neither can arise without the background of a somewhat idealized sense of connectedness with another. This necessary relationship between play and the selfobject experience is illustrated in the following story.

> The patient was a woman in her forties, who for three years had been depressed following the death of her mother. Various forms of pharmacotherapy had been unhelpful. She was the firstborn child of parents living in difficult circumstances. The next sibling, a boy, was born when the child was 18 months old. This infant contracted encephalitis and was severely disabled. The mother became totally absorbed in the rehabilitation of her son. Her daughter was employed as her helper and ally, always deferring to the needs of her brother. Her own needs were neglected. In retrospect, it seemed that the mother, who was probably depressed, replaced the transitional object in her daughter's development. The closeness she established then was never relinquished. For the rest of her life, her daughter made contact with her every day. This persisted even during the patient's marriage, which eventually failed. In thinking about her childhood, the patient felt that the parental focus upon her and the sense of stress and anxiety that pervaded the household as a result of her brother's illness had inhibited her opportunities for play. Soon after entering therapy, the patient began to paint, as if somehow aware that this may be part of the process of change. This intuition may have been compounded by reading Jung. The paintings were, initially, a series of very beautiful mandalas. Despite this activity, her progress, although steady, was not remarkable. She was chronically dysphoric. The negative mood state was anhedonic rather than despairing. Life was without pleasure or any kind of happiness. The patient, however, retained her impetus toward growth. She asked, spontaneously, that she try painting or something similar during the session. On the first occasion, she found it very difficult. The presence of the therapist seemed to act as a prohibition. She told the therapist afterwards: "It was hard because you were in the room and yet I didn't want you out of the room." She went on: "I became aware of how much on guard I am. As a child I remembered, 'Let me do it but don't look at me, don't see me,' and not really knowing whether I'm allowed to do it. And you saying I'm allowed to do it wasn't enough. It's got to come from in here."
>
> Two sessions later, however, she had a very different experience. During the session she started to fingerpaint. The following

session she described the remarkable effect this had upon her. "I felt like a light bulb had gone on—as though I could see—and feeling lighter inside—instead of darkness inside." The experience was reminiscent of the description of *fit* touched upon in Chapter 8, in which there is an almost chemical sense of enlivenment. She said: "I felt like a drug addict that can't get its supply of drugs and then it can, or it was like someone had injected me."

The elation associated with this session lasted for days. Such persistence of happiness was unexpected. She said with a giggle: "It wasn't exactly like I was on guard, but I didn't expect it to stay." The experience brought with it other changes. This was illustrated in a Tai-chi class the day following the session. The instructor made a mistake "and for the first time I was able to carry on without him." It seemed that the painting session allowed her to have some sense of an inner life, the consequence of which was an enhancement of the continuity of being, as described at the end of Chapter 11.

This session was a turning point in therapy. Rather than existing as a series of reactions to others, caught in endless busy-ness and an apparently unbreakable system of stimulus entrapment, she briefly experienced something that was her own and that, at the same time, was valued by another. However, it is important to note that she could not bring this state into being simply by a matter of will. Although we might say her initial series of mandalas was a manifestation of a drive to play, it did not work. It did not lead to the emergence of self. It was not based on a sense of inner freedom.

In his pioneering work on the significance of play, James Mark Baldwin remarked upon the child's freedom in this activity. Baldwin's theories are intriguing. He saw imitation as an early form and precursor of symbolic play. Both were seen as important in the development of consciousness of self. He anticipated many of the fundamental ideas of Winnicott, in particular the paradoxes and illusion upon which play depends.

Baldwin (1906) called the things used in play *semblant objects*. A semblant object is one "given the semblance of a sort of reality, and is treated as being such although the co-efficients of that sort of reality are lacking" (p. 110). It is to be noted that *semblance* here is what may be called *psychic semblance*, known as *self-illusion*. As Winnicott later intimated, play involves the coexistence of inner and outer. Baldwin (1906) states:

The real world, actually there, remains through the entire development, a sort of background of reference. The inner make-believe situation is developed against the background. Consciousness, even while busy with the play objects, casts sly glances behind the scenes, making sure that its firm footing of reality is not entirely lost. There is a sort of oscillation between the real and the semblant object taking place in the psychic sphere, giving an emphasized sense of "inner-outer" contrast which persists in the further genetic progressions. [p. 112]

Behind the oscillation, however, is the paradox: "The play object becomes not the inner or fancy object as such, nor yet the outer present object as such, but both at once, what we are calling the semblant object, itself the terminus of a sort of interest, which later on develops into that called 'syntelic' or contemplative" (p. 116). Baldwin here points to an affective state that accompanies play and is necessary to its going on. Without the feeling of interest, it stops. However, the feeling usually goes beyond this. It involves *einfulung*. "There is a certain *feeling-into* the given object, now made semblant of the subject's own personal feeling" (p. 122).

The child's freedom in the activity of playing is evident in two main ways. First, the child's choice of the semblant object is personal. Says Baldwin, "Play is a way of making an object for present and personal purposes, *what it might be*" (p. 124). The selection is the child's own. The object is made what the child wishes it to be. He or she can say: "This is real, or would be, but for the fact that I know it is not" (p. 112).

A second sense of freedom that invests the child's play arises in a negative way. A sense of agency is found in the child's awareness that he or she can refuse to play. The freedom might be expressed, as Baldwin put it, as "the-don't-have-to-feeling" (p. 113). Play cannot be prescribed. The woman painting mandalas had, as it were, prescribed play for herself. It could only become that form of play that involves a sense of self when a connectedness was made with the other as selfobject. The same problem surrounds an instruction to the patient to free associate. Although this may lead to virtuoso exhibitions of free association, they lead nowhere. No change occurs. What is required is spontaneous. It emerges first, in many cases, in a momentary flickering, as was seen in the session with the man with the motorcycle.

The drive to play, in people whose development has been

disrupted, is not generally manifest in the spectacular manner of the woman fingerpainting. She seemed to create within the session the main elements of transitional playing. This experience is necessary to maturation. It might be supposed that those relatively deprived of the experience during development would show, during a therapy designed to foster maturation, evidence of its emergence. This seemed so in our outcome study of thirty borderline patients (Stevenson and Meares 1992).

Modell (1963), Horton et al. (1974), and Arkema (1981) have pointed to the significance of transitional phenomena in the borderline personality. More recently, Cooper and colleagues (1985) and Morris and associates (1986) have found that borderline patients show behaviors that are soothing in a manner that has a transitional quality. It might be expected, however, that in the successful treatment of borderline subjects such behaviors would progress beyond the merely soothing. Our study (Stevenson and Meares 1992) gave some preliminary evidence in favor of this expectation.

It was discovered by chance that a number of patients had started a diary during the period of therapy. This behavior, which had not been suggested to them, seemed to be unusual for people who, in general, belonged to the less educated and lower socioeconomic section of the community. An examination of this phenomenon showed that, at least in some patients, the writing of the diary had transitional features. One patient, for example, described her experience in the following way: "I have decided to analyze why I write, as I often wonder about this. I think I know the answer. My writing saves me from myself. I am writing to you no more than I am communicating with my inner world. At times I am not me. I am outside looking on, and yet not free either, but trapped, trapped by the immobility and inability to return to be me. In yourself it is brought together so I don't fragment. If all my communication is received by one person I can be held together."

This young woman describes the anxiety-reducing effect of her writing—it stops her from fragmenting. Yet the activity is larger than this. It involves something like an inner dialogue, as if she were speaking to another part of herself, as if, in Jamesian terms, she were an *I* and *me*. At the same time, the sense of the therapist as *you* is omnipresent. The suggestion of therapist as selfobject is also suggested. "In yourself" could refer either to the patient or the therapist, or to both.

This kind of observation led to the hypothesis that those patients who used diaries or other forms of writing during their treatment would have better outcomes than those who did not. This indeed was the case. About half the patients used diaries. Although they were just as ill at the beginning of treatment, according to *DSM-III* criteria, as those who did not, their improvement after 1 year's treatment was significantly greater.

This finding supports the idea that the discovery of the experience of transitional space and the emergence of an activity analogous to the child's symbolic play are helpful in overcoming a notional arrest in personality development, which was a consequence of chronic impingement in that period of life before, say, 5 years of age. In this group of people, the drive to play was manifest in writing. However, it was manifest outside the session. This may be the usual pattern. Nevertheless, it seemed likely that whole therapeutic process, not merely the writing, was imbued with a transitional feeling. This is illustrated by the following case history.

> The patient, who was in her thirties, had been admitted to the hospital on about thirty occasions for various reasons, including quasi-psychotic episodes, self-mutilation, and attempted suicide. She had a neglectful mother and a sexually abusive father. She was intermittently afflicted with intense experiences of emptiness. During the first weeks of therapy, she clutched a small bear. The therapist learned that as a child her precious soft toys were often capriciously confiscated by her mother. Now her bedroom was filled with such toys. After about a month of therapy, the bear began to be less prominent. It was soon relegated to a handbag and later left in the patient's car. After about 12 months, it was left at home.

The transitional nature of her experience during this time was also evident in her writing. Although she did not keep a regular diary, she made notes, which had a poetic, associational quality and seemed to include a consciousness of the therapist. The nonlinear form of her writing seemed likely to be that which accompanies change, as we see later in this chapter. However, the way in which she wrote was nothing like the way she spoke in sessions. She showed nothing of the self-absorbed demeanor of the child immersed in symbolic play. This confronts us with a puzzle. If successful therapy depends upon the creation of a play space and it does not usually show itself in behaviors like painting during a session, how does it appear? We are led back to the notion of cultural space.

As we have seen, someone whose personality development has been disrupted in early life begins treatment in a characteristic manner. Such people have been damaged in a way not immediately obvious. They live almost entirely in the zone of adaption. Experience comes, overwhelmingly, from the outer world. Consequently, the story they tell deals with events, troubles, and difficulties rather than imaginings. In terms of the metaphor of the play space, they live in the real playroom.

As this story is recounted, it is apparent both to the teller and the listener that although everything in it seems relevant, sensible, and necessary to be told, it is, in some fundamental way, entirely unsatisfactory. Such a historical record of an individual life, although real in terms of the happenings described, does not *feel* real. It seems to be about things going on outside. The task is to help this person discover another reality, which is personal and which comes from within. Again, in terms of the metaphor, the aim is to create the play space. It will not, however, be the same play space as that of the transitional child. It does not generally appear in the clear form expressed by the woman who finger-painted, but covertly. Essential features of its emergence are illustrated in the following, rather typical story.

> The patient is a woman in her fifties who has had a very hard life. The poverty of her parents caused her to be placed in an orphanage in a country town at the age of 3. She stayed there until she was 10. She had intermittent care from an aunt and after this, little schooling, then factory work. Over the years she was sexually exploited in various ways. She is now married, with two children, and the presentation is because of an intractable depression, not treatable by medication.
>
> Her characteristic conversation with her therapist is about the difficulties of her life. The accounts of these problems are interspersed with a mirthless laugh, which seems to have the purpose, not of registering amusement, but of engaging the therapist. Each session she comes with a different catalog of symptoms. The therapist constantly seeks to understand and respond to her immediate experience. After some months, a change begins to

occur in her life. Instead of orienting herself entirely outward, toward others, she now thinks of her own development. She decides to take a course of study. Some weeks after this, she starts the session with the unexpected news that she feels well. Soon she is talking about issues in her course that interest her. They are, first, women's issues and then, language. Imperceptibly, she moves to the story of the maltreatment of the Australian aboriginal population by the white settlers. She then discusses a newspaper account of a disadvantaged man who has succeeded in a social sense. Her story then moves again, without clear linking, to the orphanage at night. She is lying awake and hearing a cow bellowing out in the fields. Then she said, "I seem to have lost the point. I wonder why I thought of the cow just then."

The point of this story is that she has not lost the point but has started to find it. The past is there in her story, but it has an unusual aliveness. She is not telling the therapist something like "I often felt lonely in the night at the orphanage." The past is with her in the present. Moreover, the image of a bellowing cow, who perhaps has lost her calf, and the related one of the little girl who cannot sleep evoke echoes of isolation and coldness, implying layers of associations in the manner of poetry or dream.

What has happened in this session? First, great changes have come about. One of the most important cannot be shown in a transcript. Whereas the therapist has for months had to overcome the feeling of boredom in the face of the endless clamor of everyday life thrust upon him by his patient, he feels differently during this session. A feeling of interest is aroused, which, by the time the memory of the orphanage at night is reached, becomes compelling. We are reminded of the observations of Baldwin and Winnicott regarding the affect of interest associated with play. This, itself, is associated with the patient's unusual state of well-being.

A second change involves the form of the conversation. In the past, her thought was undeviating, as if caught on a tramline, concerned with the ceaseless quotidian. In this session, the account is nonlinear. It is made up of a series of episodes, which Barthes (1975) might call lexias[2] and which superficially may not be connected. Nevertheless, they are clearly linked. The movements between them are smooth, not made by jumps or sudden changes of topic. She touches upon what it is to be a woman, the significance of language, the maltreatment of a deprived group, the struggle of an outcast, the loneliness of an abandoned child. These various episodes arise from something more fundamental, which underlies them. They all derive from the personal reality of a woman who has never been properly responded to and who has found no words to express what is essentially her own private experience. In this session, the therapist, who admired the woman's courage, is rewarded for his patient efforts over months to put in words what he has understood of her feelings and personal world. The mental activity that underlies play has been activated. What is evident, however, is not the behavior of the transitional child at play, but something different. Instead of occupying, in an experiential sense, social space or the adaptive zone, the patient has moved into cultural space, in which two forms of mental activity are working together. Public and private are co-ordinated, as described in Chapter 7. This results in a change in language.

When the form of the session changes so that it is no longer linear, it signals that the private or inner language is breaking into the linear speech of social discourse. Two dimensions of speech, which correspond with the two playrooms, intersect and are manifest in a conversation in which there are discrepancies, strange intrusions, unexpected memories, and apparent condensations, perhaps expressed as metaphor or in an unusual word. In the same way that the experience conveyed in the words of a poem cannot easily be described in prose, the drift of images, feelings, ideas, and memories that sometimes go on within us cannot be directly converted into the language of the social world. The difficulty involved in the expression of an inner life was remarked upon by Wilhelm Stekel (1924) in the following way: "This discrepancy between speech and thought, or rather between what we want to say and what we can say, is due mainly to the fact that we never have single thoughts but always many, an entire polyphony, of which speech expresses but one melody; the other voices and the counterpoint remain hidden" (p. 313).

The nascent self in therapy may be obscured or overlaid by a form of language that is not designed to portray it but rather to communicate with others. The therapist's goal is to discern within social speech and the form of language built for discourse with the outer world the embedded elements of another kind of speech through which self can be visualized. He or she can only do so by maintaining Freud's state of evenly hovering attention, in which no particular element of the conversation is fastened upon.[3] Furthermore, the therapist's contributions should have something of the character of inner speech so that they enrich the nonlinear form of mental activity rather than trigger a return to the language of adaption. The therapist might make remarks that contribute to linking of experiences. He or she attends to metaphor, which is often embedded, since the image it contains may open into larger areas of psychic life. Most importantly, the therapist maintains as far as possible a capacity to view the experience that arises in the encounter and that patient and therapist jointly try to describe. Through the maintenance of this duality, the therapist helps to foster its achievement in the patient.

Essentially, the therapist's state of mind should resemble that to which the patient's should be moving. He or she should be using imagination, and in a particular way, not *on* the unfolding experience, but *in* it. However, the therapist should not inflict his or her own order upon what is being discovered. The task is not to make it logical or orderly.[4]

The change that comes about when a connectedness is made, when the patient is able to use the therapist as a selfobject, is profound, not only in terms of the shape of the conversation, but also in terms of a feeling of well-being. Anais Nin (1931–1934) described it. During her first analysis she felt dissatisfaction and boredom: "With Allendy, I became aware that each thing I did fell into its expected places; I became aware of the monotony of the design, I experienced a kind of discouragement with the banality of life and character, the logical chain reaction of cliches. He discovered only the skeleton which resembled other skeletons" (p. 288). With Allendy she was in the grip of linear thought. "Rather than enter this ordinary life, which was death to my imagination" (p. 282), she ended her association with Allendy. After this, she entered treatment with Otto Rank. The experience was very different. She wrote:

> There is a most baffling thing about analysis which is a challenge to a writer. It is almost impossible to detect the links by which one arrives at a certain statement. There is a fumbling, a shadowy area. One does not arrive suddenly at the clear-cut phrases I put down. There were hesitancies, innuendoes, detours. I reported it as a limpid dialogue, but left out the shadows and obscurities. One cannot give a progressive development [p. 76]

. . . . I stopped for a moment to search for the order and progression of our talks, but these talks follow a capricious association pattern which is elusive. The order made in reality, chronological, is another matter entirely. [p. 290]

Their talks had the elusive, capricious, associative shape of the flow of inner life. She remarked, "Analysis has to do with flow. I am flowing again" (1939–1944, p. 214). This experience contrasts with the sense of stagnation and atomization of those with disorders of self.

A change has come about that is analogous to the child's move from the real playroom to that which involves illusion. Activity is no longer, as Piaget put it, *"adaption to reality,* but on the contrary, assimilation of *reality to self"* (Gruber and Vonèche 1977, p. 492). The manifestation of this experience, however, is no longer evident in its relatively pure form, which, with its condensations of language, its associational quality and its improbabilities, resembles the structure of a dream (see Chapter 6). Rather, in cultural space, it has its effect below the surface, breaking it up. When in a session, an inner or private language begins to show itself, it has a nonlinear form, altering the patterns of secondary process. Rather than a seamless narrative, one can look back upon the session and see that it was made up of a number of apparently disparate stories, reflecting an underlying flux of images, feelings, and memories.

In conclusion, the patient's need to discover a personal reality is manifest in a drive to play. It is the therapist's task to somehow liberate this activity, the movements of which resemble those of the dream. In those with disorders of self, its first manifestations are brief and largely hidden in the linear language of adaption.

The emergence, however, of a nonlinear form of mental life is insufficient in itself. Although moments of reverie may be useful at times, they have no potential for growth. In order to become real, the shifting affect-laden shapes of an inner world must be represented. Since it cannot be seen, an empathic imagination, or *fantasia* as Vico called it, is required. Re-presentation, however, is not the thing itself. Something new is created. Each attempt, each movement across the space of the *I* and *me,* is another step in the enlargement of self.

NOTES

1. PLAY AND THE SENSE OF SELF

1. Strachey (1961, p. 8) pointed out that Freud did not clearly distinguish between ego and self until late in his life. Hartmann (1939) is seen as the pioneer of "the conceptual separation of the self from the ego" (Kohut 1971, p. xiii).

2. Picabia was a star of the Armory Show of 1913, a highly influential exhibition in New York, which presented European art to an American audience (Borras 1985). Malevic portrayed people constructed of cones and cylinders at about the same time as Leger produced very similar machine-like images (Gray 1986).

3. The idea that these men formed a loose intellectual grouping is illustrated by the index to an authoritative anthology of Piaget's work (Gruber and Vonèche 1977). Only six people are referred to more than ten times. Edward Claparède is one of them. He founded the Rousseau Institute in Geneva, which he eventually turned over to his pupil, Piaget. Claparède had a close intellectual relationship with Baldwin, who is also one of the six. Baldwin was a friend of Janet. It is intriguing to learn that at their first meeting, since neither spoke the native

language of the other, they resorted to Latin (Ellenberger 1970). Janet was also a close friend of Bergson, who was his advocate for a professorship at the College de France. Both men are among the six to whom Piaget referred most. The other two are his colleague, Barbel Inhelder, and Freud, with whom Piaget conducted a somewhat wary debate. It is of interest that the five honorary members elected on the formation of the American Psychopathological Association in 1910 were Claparède, Janet, Jung, Forel, and Freud.

4. This incident is recounted in Meares 1976, 1977.

5. James Mark Baldwin (1906) was perhaps the first to put forward the idea that play is an important factor in human development. He anticipated many of the ideas of D. W. Winnicott (see Chapter 18). Johan Huizinga (1938) was also a pioneer of the view that play is important. He wrote: "It is a *significant* function—that is to say, there is some sense to it. In play there is something 'at play' which transcends the immediate needs of life and imparts meaning to the action" (p. 19). He assumed "that play must serve something which is *not* play, that it must have some biological purpose" (p. 20).

2. THE SECRET

1. Another means of determining the age at which the conceptualization of an inner world is achieved includes the study of false belief. For example, children are shown a box of Smarties (candies). When the children open it, they find it contains pencils. The pencils are then put back in the box and the children are asked what another child who has not yet seen the box will think is inside it. Three-year-olds tend to say pencils (Gopnik and Astington 1988, Perner et al. 1987). The children respond as if there is nothing they know that other people do not know.

2. Jung (1961) remarked that "there is no better means of intensifying the treasured feeling of individuality than the possession of a secret which the individual is pledged to guard" (p. 342). Jung noted the importance of the act of secrecy in his own life, telling of a carved manikin he kept hidden in an attic. This episode "formed the climax, the conclusion" of his childhood (p. 22).

3. R. St. Barbe Baker (1970). The quotation comes from a broadcast on the Australian Broadcasting Commission in 1980. His account of the soothing nature of his "Madonna of the Woods" is echoed by Jung (1961) in his description of his manikin. "In all difficult situations, whenever I

had done something wrong or my feelings had been hurt, or when my father's irritability or my mother's invalidism oppressed me, I thought of my carefully bedded-down and wrapped-up manikin and his smooth, prettily colored stone. From time to time—often at intervals of weeks— I secretly stole up to the attic when I could be certain that no one would see me . . . I contented myself with the feeling of newly won security, and was satisfied to possess something that no one knew and no one could get at. It was an inviolable secret which must never be betrayed, for the safety of my life depended on it. Why that was so I did not ask myself. It simply was so" (pp. 21–22).

3. SELF AS DOUBLE

1. Freud (1939) described a mechanism that conducts an interplay between inner and outer worlds and operates as a complex decision-processing system. It is a conception that is larger than the *I*, for it determines not only consciousness, but also unconsciousness. However, it should not include the contents of consciousness. It contains nothing, neither memories, ideas, nor sensory impressions.

4. *I* AND THE OTHER

1. Zigmond et al. (1973). Konishi (1985) says that the study of birdsong has made significant contributions to the development of modern ethology and that it has raised the controversial issue of instinct versus learning from the realm of semantic discourse and confusion to an experimentally tractable subject.

2. Locke and Pearson (1990) describe the effects of deprivation of babbling. A child who had been tracheotomized was generally aphonic between the ages of 0.5–1.8. She was cognitively and socially normal, with near normal comprehension of language. Following decannulation, her utterances revealed a tenth of the canonical syllables that might be expected in normally developing infants. In this way, she was like a congenitally deaf child. Two months later (1.10), she produced only a handful of different words. It seems possible that hearing one's own babbling is a necessary precursor to the attainment of language.

3. Young (1974). McLean (1986) remarks that the behaviors of nursing and maternal care, together with audiovocal communication for maintaining maternal–offspring contact, are forms of behavior that clearly mark the evolutionary dividing line between reptiles and mam-

mals. He believes these behaviors are related to the activity of cingulate gyrus and its subcortical connections. This system has no recognizable counterpart in the reptilian brain.

5. THE ROLE OF TOYS

1. It is important to emphasize that the discussion here concerns conception rather than perception. The child of 3 years does not *experience* others as knowing of his or her inner states; he or she merely *believes* it. In this way is distinguished the putative world of the schizophrenic from that of the normally developing child.

6. TWO PLAYROOMS

1. Sorce and Emde (1981). Matas, Arend, and Sroufe (1978) found that infants who were securely attached at 18 months showed a significantly greater amount of symbolic play at 24 months than those less securely attached.

2. The child's relative lack of a sense of ownership of his or her core experiences can be seen as the basis of the normal separation anxiety that is manifest between the ages of 6–7 months and 4 years (Meares 1986). This explanation of separation anxiety is complementary to the Kleinian thesis, which depends upon the imagined power of the child's wishes. Both ideas can be derived from the more fundamental notion that before the age of 4, or thereabouts, the child does not conceive of an inner world.

3. Baldwin (1897). His concept is related to Kohut's in that imitation, which is an aspect of mirroring, is central to it. In Baldwin's description, however, the imitation is in the reverse direction. "My sense of myself grows by imitation of you, and my sense of yourself grows in terms of myself" (p. 338). A reciprocal responsiveness is suggested in descriptions such as those of Trevarthen (1983).

4. Studies such as those of Herman et al. (1989), Zanarini et al. (1989), Ludolph et al. (1990) suggest that very many people diagnosed as borderline in adult life were subjected to verbal, physical, or sexual abuse in childhood. The model for the development of borderline personality advanced here is consistent with Pine's "Borderline-

Child-to-be" (1986). He states that the child who is destined to become borderline has had early experiences that have an effect equivalent to the creation of "too much noise in the psychic system" (p. 452).

7. FRAGMENTS OF SPACE AND OF SELF

1. Amsterdam (1972) borrowed a technique used by Gallup (1970), working with chimpanzees, to chart the development of self-recognition in infants. The children's noses were surreptitiously dabbed with rouge. The infants were then placed before a mirror and asked "See" and "Who's that?" They were considered to show self-recognition when they pointed to the discrepancy of the red spot. Lewis and Brooks-Gunn (1979) further developed the "red spot" strategy in a systematic way, using mirrors, photographs, and videotapes. They showed that infants first clearly recognized themselves in a mirror between the ages of 15–18 months. By 21 to 24 months, children are able to recognize photographs of themselves, using their names and appropriate personal pronouns.

2. Many authors (e.g., Kail 1984, Nelson 1984) discuss the development of infant memory in terms of recognition and recall memory. Recognition is considered more primitive, or less sophisticated, than recall memory and is evident at an earlier age. In recognition, a stimulus is actually present and the individual has only to decide if it is familiar or not; in recall, the stimulus is absent and so must be recovered from memory. The emergence of recall memory is a major milestone in the cognitive development of the infant, since the emergence of recall abilities is necessary to the development of a conceptual system, the formation of symbols to refer to these concepts, and a representational system. The age at which recall and its associated abilities are achieved, however, is a matter of great debate. Piaget (cited Mandler 1984) suggested that the development of these abilities occurred toward the end of the sensorimotor period of early childhood, around 18 to 24 months of age, but this has been disputed now by a number of theorists (e.g., Ashmead and Perlmutter 1980, Mandler 1984, Olson and Strauss 1984).

Recognition memory is apparent in the first days of life when, for example, the infant appears to recognize his or her mother's voice (De Casper and Fifer 1980). Between the ages of 2 months and 5 months, recognition memory matures with increasing complexity and retention of the information involved (Kail 1984).

The earliest evidence of true recall is about the age of 7 to 8 months (Mandler 1984). Recall, however, is a complex idea and has different forms. They include incidental recall and intentional recall. The former is present when an environmental cue evokes a memory of an object or event connected with that cue. For example, the smell of coffee reminds us of an incident in a coffee shop. *Incidental recall* is the most frequently occurring type of recall. It is the core of our continuing sense of going on being (Arnold 1984).

The type of recall most commonly studied in laboratory situations is *intentional recall* (also called deliberate recall and explicit recall). For instance, a subject is asked to remember a list of words, then recall them after an interval. We use intentional recall when taking exams. There is very little data on the types of recall in infancy, but it would appear that incidental recall, that is, recall through being reminded, emerges before intentional (either externally or self-instigated) recall. Mandler (1984) states that 2 years is the earliest age for which there is evidence of intentional recall, although it is not made clear whether this is because there is no evidence for recall before this age, or because it has not been investigated before this age.

Investigations of the memorial capacities of children are complicated by the possibility that very different results might be obtained when the child is in the home rather than in a laboratory. It seems necessary, therefore, to devise natural conditions for these investigations.

The differences in recall ability shown between experimental situations is highlighted in the following study on 21- and 26-month-old children (DeLoache 1980). Each child was given three experimental situations in counterbalanced order. (1) A toy (Big Bird) was placed in one of four unmarked boxes in the middle of the floor (in the child's home). (2) Big Bird was placed in one of four plain boxes that were situated next to an identifiable piece of furniture (a potential landmark). (3) Big Bird was hidden (in full view of the child, as in the other conditions) somewhere in the house but not in one of the boxes. After a set interval, the child was to find Big Bird. The overall results showed that the third, most natural condition (anywhere in the house) resulted in the most successful retrieval of Big Bird for both age groups. Older children (and not younger children) were able to utilize the landmark cues, and in fact there was no difference obtained for the landmark (second) condition and the natural (third) condition. Similar results were found in a study using unmarked boxes, boxes with picture cues on the lids (instead of placement near furniture), and the natural environment (the room or house) (DeLoache and Brown 1983). Ashmead and Perlmutter (1980), taking naturalistic studies one step further, asked parents to keep a diary of instances where the child (aged 7, 9, or 11 months) demonstrated any form of memory (whether it was recognition or recall). From this it was established that children as young as 7 months were capable of recall memory, mainly recall for object location. Younger infants (7 and 9 months) tended to search for objects with permanent locations, whereas 11-month-olds also looked for objects in temporary locations. Location of objects with permanent locations were generally associated with particular behavior patterns, such as the cereal cupboard being associated with food and eating.

What is remembered changes with maturation. Nelson and Ross (1980) found that for children of 21 months, the location of objects and people make up the majority of memory instances. For children who were 26 months, memory of events and episodes became more important.

This kind of evidence shows that by about the age of 2, the child has recall abilities. However, it is probable that recall abilities are present earlier. This is suggested by studies of deferred imitation, that is, the capacity to reproduce, or mimic, the behavior of another person when that person is no longer present. Meltzoff (1988) has found imitation occurring 1 week after the modeling event in 14-month-old children. It would be consistent with object permanence data if recall were shown to be established by 18 months.

8. FIT AND SELF-ESTEEM

1. For a review, see Harter (1983). She quotes Wylie's assessment (1979) of the significance of much of the data in this field.
2. This term was introduced by Wilhelm Wundt (1904) and his pupil Edward Titchener (1905). It fell into disuse following the demise of the introspectionist school of psychology. It has now been reinstated.
3. See Eibl-Eibesfeldt (1970), Izard (1971), Ekman et al. (1972).

9. BODY FEELING AND DISJUNCTION

1. This constellation of observations is termed the *orienting response* (see Sokolov 1960).
2. Individuals whose personal reality does not match the responses

of others may become afflicted with derealization. Adolescents may be particularly vulnerable (Meares and Grose 1978).

3. In severe psychiatric illness, the capacity to habituate to redundant stimuli is gravely impaired, (e.g., Horvath, Friedman, and Meares 1980, Horvath and Meares 1979, Meares and Horvath 1972). Certain drugs, notably nicotine, (Friedman, Horvath, and Meares 1974) enhance habituation, presumably contributing to their reinforcing properties. This effect helps to explain the extraordinary intake of nicotine by some schizophrenics.

4. Winnicott (1953) repeatedly spoke of the value of the parent's *failure* of adaption. This was necessarily preceded by a relatively complete adaption so that normal omnipotence is allowed to arise. "Good enough mothering is natural, and involves both attunement and failure" (p. 10).

5. The intersubjectivity of the therapeutic relationship has been extensively explored by Atwood and colleagues (e.g., Atwood and Stolorow 1984, Stolorow, Brandchaft, and Atwood 1987).

10. REVERSALS

1. Klein (1955). Previous to the more recent evolution of a psychology of self, ideas derived from the work of Melanie Klein were used to explain the shifting self state of the borderline personality. Kernberg (e.g., 1975, 1984) is the most prominent of those theorists who understand the phenomena of severe personality disorder in terms of the defenses of splitting and projective identification. Kernberg (1968) has observed what appears characteristic of borderline patients, that is, "a rapid oscillation between moments of projection of a self-representation while the patient remains identified with the corresponding object-representation, and other moments in which it is the object-representation that is projected while the object identifies with the corresponding self-representation" (p. 605). Kernberg (1968) gives an example that makes clear that this oscillation conforms to what I call a reversal. He describes a situation in which "a primitive, sadistic mother image may be projected into the therapist while the patient experiences himself as the frightened, attacked, panic-stricken little child; moments later, the patient may experience himself as the stern, prohibitive, moralistic (and extremely sadistic) primitive mother image, while the therapist is seen as the guilty, defensive, frightened but rebellious child"

(p. 605). This oscillation is seen to arise through projective identification called upon to externalize aggressive self and object images. Kernberg has retained the essence of these early views in his later writings.

The concept of projective identification as it is currently described (e.g., Goldstein 1991) has a number of difficulties. They are beyond the scope of this book. Thomas Ogden (1982) has authoritatively reviewed this field.

2. Meares and Hobson (1977). Brandchaft (1983) points out that the deterioration in the patient's psychic state that sometimes occurs during psychotherapy has traditionally been conceived as part of the patient's individual psychopathology, whereas the origin of the negative therapeutic reaction can often be found in the intersubjective field.

3. Stolorow and Atwood (1992) note that grandiose

fantasies are constructed reactively in situations wherein the child's primary affective experiences of excitement, expansiveness, pride, efficacy and pleasure in himself fail to evoke the requisite validating responsiveness from caregivers. The concrete imagery of the grandiose fantasy both dramatizes and affirms the unvalidated affective experience and depicts as well what the child perceived was required of him in order to extract the missing responsiveness. [pp. 61–62]

11. STIMULUS ENTRAPMENT

1. Plaut (1966) gave an early account of this state. Modell (1976) described the effect of the patient's stimulus entrapment on the therapist. He considered the patient's state a consequence of the failure of the "holding environment," using Winnicott's language.

2. The idea that a zone of silence beyond impingement is needed in order to discover a sense of being is expressed in different ways in the work of Samuel Beckett (Meares 1973a).

13. THE MASK

1. Freud's concept of libido has been heavily criticized in recent years. Nevertheless, certain elements that are essential to it seem important. Consequently the *hedonic tone* of Wundt (1904) has been

reintroduced. The concept might perhaps be recast using biological evidence such as that of Olds and Milner (1954). Lichtenberg has pioneered an attempt to base psychoanalytic concepts of motivation on recent biological and child developmental data. The sense of "me-ness" of James (1892) and Claparède (1911) may be related to a certain kind of hedonic tone.

2. Winnicott's paper of 1960 touches on each but gives the impression there is only one form of the phenomenon. This is evident in such remarks as: "The False Self has one positive and very important function: to hide the True Self, which it does by compliance with environmental demands" (pp. 146–147).

14. BEGINNING AGAIN

1. The *DSM-III-R* criteria are arranged in order to show this relationship. There are eight criteria. The *DSM-III-R* ordering is given in parens and the criteria briefly considered in turn.

1:(6) "Marked and persistent identity disturbance manifested by uncertainty about at least two of the following: self-image, sexual orientation, long-term goals or career choice, type of friends desired, preferred values." This is the central feature. In this item, the word *identity* is used instead of self. This, in my view, is a mistake. *Self* and *identity* are not synonymous, as we have seen. Indeed, identity is often exaggerated or given undue importance where the sense of self is precarious or nebulous.

2:(8) "Frantic efforts to avoid real or imagined abandonment." The sense of going-on-being depends upon the other as selfobject. For this reason, the efforts to maintain the connection with the other are often truly frantic.

3:(7) "Chronic feelings of emptiness or boredom." Emptiness and boredom are different. Emptiness can be conceived in terms of the play space. When those circumstances that make inner experience possible are lost, the child, as it were, faces a vacant room. The same may be said for those with disorders of self. The break with the selfobject brings with it an emptiness that is more than mere vacancy. Since what has vanished is going-on-being, what is left will be pain, fear, even annihilation. The individual now feels without substance and the diminishment of the sense of existence is felt in the totality of self, including the body. Boredom, which in severe form is experienced as deadness, is a consequence of the false self system, in which a measure of connectedness with the other involves a sacrifice of personal and emotional reality. Reality is stifled and the sense of authentic lived experience lost.

4:(2) "Impulsiveness in at least two areas that are potentially self-damaging, e.g., spending, sex, substance abuse, shoplifting, reckless driving, binge eating." The pain of emptiness is such that those affected try to fill it. There is a search for stimuli, which may be manifest in busy-ness. More extreme measures involve the infliction of pain. Drinking and drugs also help to fill an experiential void. Some of these behaviors do more than fill emptiness with sensation. They attempt to maintain the integrity of self through symbolically retaining a sense of connection with the lost selfobject.

5:(3) "Affective instability: marked shifts from baseline mood to depression, irritability, or anxiety, usually lasting a few hours and only rarely more than a few days." Since the borderline depends for his or her sense of existence upon the other, variations in this relationship, even of a subtle kind, may provoke profound changes and apparently inexplicable changes in mood.

6:(4) "Inappropriate, intense anger or lack of control of anger, e.g., frequent displays of temper, constant anger, recurrent physical fights." Although small disjunctions between self and selfobject may result in transient mood changes, larger breaks might precipitate sudden anger. Also, responses from others that seem to devalue, and in this way attack, essential aspects of a personal reality may be sensed as a physical assault, provoking rage and occasionally actual violence.

7:(5) "Recurrent suicidal threats, gestures, or behavior, or self-mutilating behavior." The result of varying combinations of intense futility, despair, annihilation, and the sense of abandonment.

8:(1) "A pattern of unstable and intense interpersonal relationships characterized by alternating between extremes of overidealization and devaluation." This item refers to attitudes adopted toward significant others. Idealization is part of the experience of the other as selfobject; devaluation follows the loss of this experience. However, these are only two of the many aspects of the other that are linked to the shifting multiplicity of selves manifest in the severe personality disorder. The type of severe personality disorder identified as borderline is part of a larger grouping of personality disorder that includes the narcissistic and histrionic. The names are historically determined and most unsuitable. All three describe manifestations of disruptions of the same system. The borderline is the least stable and the histrionic the most, with narcissistic occupying an intermediate position. Depending on the interchange with social environment the individual can fluctuate between these diagnostic categories, even in a single session, as described by Brandchaft and Stolorow (1984).

The *DSM-III-R* catalog of histrionic traits describes, in essence, an individual who is constantly behaving so as to elicit mirroring responses from others. The narcissistic personality description highlights a variant of item 8 of the borderline description. With devaluation of others comes an overvaluation of self. These two descriptions are not discussed in detail since they are "first-generation" catalogs, likely to be revised.

2. Crafoord (1977) describes day-hospital treatments for borderline patients in which the institution takes on transitional qualities.

3. Freud (1920–1922) suggested that the therapist "surrender himself to his own unconscious mental activity, in a state of evenly suspended attention, to avoid so far as possible, reflection and the construction of conscious expectations, not to try to fix anything that he hears particularly in his memory, and by these means to catch the drift of the patient's unconscious with his own unconscious" (p. 239). Schwaber (1983) points out the significance of this remark in her description of the listening stance of the therapist.

4. Winnicott (1974). In this passage (pp. 101–102), he describes a change in his technique over two decades. He attests to the realization that the natural process that develops in the therapeutic situation should not be broken up by interpretations. He now sees that in the past deep change had been prevented or delayed in certain patients by his need to interpret. He now finds more joy in waiting for the patient's own discovery than he once did in being clever. His interpretations show the patient the limits of the therapist's understanding.

16. EMPATHY AND DECENTRATION

1. McLean (1986) makes this point from the neurophysiological point of view, suggesting that play is associated with the cingulate limbic cortex.

2. Meares (1983). Kohut's paper (1959) focuses on the metaphoric observation that empathy involves.

3. Olinick (1984) writes on the distinction between sympathy and empathy.

4. Stern (1985) reviews several reports of this phenomenon.

5. Although the first evidence of empathy is found early in life, it is a capacity that enlarges with maturation. There is, for example, a sudden growth in empathic awareness during adolescence. A continuing growth in the capacity to understand the feelings and personal worlds of others throughout life enables one, ideally, to deal with the process of dying in a way that shows empathy with those who survive (Meares 1981).

17. ERROR AND THE TRANSFERENCE

1. Kohut (1984) regarded his concepts of *optimal frustration* and *transmuting internalization* as central to his therapeutic method and to his ideas about therapeutic change.

2. Freud (1914). Edgar Levenson (1972), whom Lifton (1976) has seen as the herald of the recent paradigm shift, has repeatedly pointed out the significance of this remark.

3. Rather than being a means to the discovery of the pathogenic secret, the achievement of an associative form of mental function is seen as a therapeutic end in itself. This is consistent with a study of group function, which suggested that groups in which linear, logical thought patterns dominated were unlikely to be therapeutic (Meares 1973b). It is also consistent with the thesis of Kris (1983), who wrote that the free association process "deliberately describes the analyst's goal in the use of the free association method as the enhancement of the patient's free associations and not as the production of insight, nor as the development of a regressive transference neurosis and its resolution, nor as the reduction of symptoms and of suffering" (p. 3).

4. The notion of structuralization implies organization and integration of previously disconnected pieces of experience. It is suggested that associative form of mental function is necessary to this process (Meares 1977, 1990).

5. This kind of secret is quite different from the pathogenic secret (Meares 1987). It might, perhaps, be called *the generative secret*.

18. A DRIVE TO PLAY

1. Lichtenberg (1989), in suggesting a new approach to motivation in psychoanalysis, proposed an explorative-assertive system, which involves curiosity and includes symbolic play.

2. Barthes (1975) broke up a Balzac novella

> into a series of brief, contiguous fragments, which we shall call lexias, since they are units of reading. . . . The lexia will include sometimes a few words, sometimes several sentences; it is a matter of convenience: it will suffice that the lexia be the best possible space in which we can observe meanings; its dimension, empirically determined, will depend on the density of connotations, variable according to the moments of the text: all we require is that each lexia should have at most three or four meanings to be enumerated. [p. 13]

3. Freud (1920–1922) p. 239.
4. Winnicott (1974) was critical of the orderly therapist, whose aim was to translate the patient's productions into the language of adaption, or secondary process. He wrote about this issue in several ways. An example follows:

> Free association that reveals a coherent theme is already affected by anxiety, and the cohesion of ideas is a defence organization. Perhaps it is to be accepted that there are patients who at times need the therapist to note the nonsense that belongs to the mental state of the individual at rest without the need even for the patient to communicate this nonsense, that is to say, without the need for the patient to organize nonsense. Organized nonsense is already a defence, just as organized chaos is a denial of chaos. The therapist who cannot take this communication becomes engaged in a futile attempt to find some organization in the nonsense, as a result of which the patient leaves the nonsense area because of the hopelessness about communicating nonsense. [p. 65]

REFERENCES

Abraham, K. (1924). A short study of the development of the libido, viewed in the light of mental disorders. In *Selected Papers of Karl Abraham*, ed. E. Jones. London: Hogarth, 1949.

Als, H., Tronick, E., Lester, B., and Brazelton, T. B. (1977). The Brazelton Neonatal Behavioural Assessment Scale. *Journal of Abnormal Child Psychology* 5:215–231.

Amsterdam, B. (1972). Mirror self image reactions before age two. *Developmental Psychology* 5:297–305.

Anisfeldt, M. (1984). *Language Development from Birth to Three*. Hillsdale, NJ: Lawrence Erlbaum.

Arkema, P. (1981). The borderline personality and transitional relatedness. *American Journal of Psychiatry* 138:172–177.

Arlow, J. (1985). Interpretation and psychoanalytic psychotherapy. In *The Transference in Psychotherapy: Clinical Management*, ed. E. A. Schwaber. New York: International Universities Press.

Armstrong, D. (1981). *The Nature of Mind*. New York: Cornell University Press.

Arnold, M. B. (1984). *Memory and the Brain*. Hillsdale, NJ: Lawrence Erlbaum.

Ashmead, D. H., and Perlmutter, M. (1980). Infant memory in everyday life. In *Children's Memory: New Directions for Child Development*, no. 10, ed. M. Perlmutter. San Francisco: Jossey-Bass.

Atwood, G., and Stolorow, R. (1984). *Structures of Subjectivity*. Hillsdale, NJ: Analytic Press.

Baldwin, J. M. (1897). *Mental Development in the Child and the Race*. New York: Macmillan.

―――― (1906). *Thoughts and Things: or Genetic Logic*. Vol. 1. London: Macmillan.

Barthes, R. (1975). *S/Z*. Trans. R. Miller. London: Cape.

Bayer, T., Baer, P., and Early, C. (1991). Situational and psychophysiological factors in psychologically induced pain. *Pain* 44:45-50.

Beebe, B., and Lachmann, F. (1988). Mother–infant influence and precursors of psychic structure. In *Frontiers in Self Psychology: Progress in Self Psychology*, vol. 3, ed. A. Goldberg. Hillsdale, NJ: Analytic Press.

Beecher, H. K. (1966). Pain: one mystery solved. *Science* 151:840-841.

Berlin, I. (1977). *Vico and Herder: Two Studies in the History of Ideas*. New York: Vintage.

Borras, M. L. (1985). *Picabia*. New York: Rizzoli.

Bower, T. (1971). The object in the world of the infant. *Scientific American* 225:30-38.

―――― (1974). *Development in Infancy*. San Francisco: Freeman.

Brandchaft, B. (1983). The negativism of the negative therapeutic reaction and the psychology of self. In *The Future of Psychoanalysis*, ed. A. Goldberg. New York: International Universities Press.

Brandchaft, B., and Stolorow, R. (1984). The borderline concept: pathological character or iatrogenic myth? In *Empathy*, vol. 2, ed. J. Lichtenberg, M. Bornstein, and D. Silver. Hillsdale, NJ: Analytic Press.

Brazelton, T. B., Tronick, E. C., Adamson, L., et al. (1975). Early mother–infant reciprocity. In *The Parent–Infant Interaction*, ed. M. Hofer and R. Porter. Amsterdam: Excerpta Medica.

Breuer, J., and Freud, S. (1895). Studies in hysteria. *Standard Edition* 2.

Brill, A. A. (1937). Introduction. In *Studies in Hysteria* by J. Breuer and S. Freud, trans. A. A. Brill. New York: Nervous and Mental Disorders Monograph no. 61.

Brown, G., Andrews, B., Harris, T., et al. (1986). Social support, self-esteem and depression. *Psychological Medicine* 16:813-831.

Bruner, J. (1983). *Child Talk: Learning to Use Language*. New York: Norton.

Buss, A. H. (1980). *Self-Consciousness and Social Anxiety*. San Francisco: Freeman.

Carpenter, G. (1974). Mother's face and the newborn. *New Scientist* 61:742.

Claparède, E. (1911). Recognition and "me-ness." In *Organization and Pathology of Thought: Selected Sources*, ed. D. Rapaport. New York: Columbia University Press, 1951.

Cooley, C. (1902). *Human Nature and the Social Order.* New York: Scribner.

Cooper, S., Perry, J., Hoke, L., et al. (1985). Transitional relatedness and borderline personality disorder. *Psychoanalytic Psychology* 2:114–128.

Coopersmith, S. (1967). *The Antecedents of Self Esteem.* San Francisco: Freeman.

Cornwall, A., and Donderi, D. (1988). The effect of experimentally induced anxiety on the experience of pressure pain. *Pain* 35:105–113.

Crafoord, C. (1977). Day hospital treatment for borderline patients: the institution as transitional object. In *Borderline Personality Disorders*, ed. P. Hartocollis. New York: International Universities Press.

Craig, K. (1984). Emotional aspects of pain. In *Textbook of Pain*, ed. P. Wall and R. Melzack. Edinburgh: Churchill Livingstone.

Darwin, C. R. (1872). *The Expression of Emotions in Man and Animals.* Abridged edition. London: Watts, 1934.

de Beauvoir, S. (1969). *A Very Easy Death.* Trans. P. O'Brian. London: Penguin.

De Casper, A. J., and Fifer, W. P. (1980). Of human bonding: newborns prefer their mother's voices. *Science* 208:1174–1176.

DeLoache, J. S. (1980). Naturalistic studies of memory for object location in very young children. In *Children's Memory: New Directions for Child Development*, no. 10, ed. M. Perlmutter. San Francisco: Jossey-Bass.

DeLoache, J. S., and Brown, A. (1983). Very young children's memory for the location of objects in a large scale environment. *Child Development* 54:888–897.

Deltaglia, L. (1990). Victims and perpetrators of sexual abuse: a psychosocial study from France. *Child Abuse and Neglect* 14:445–447.

Descartes, R. (1637–1641). *Discourse on Method and the Meditations.* Trans. F. Sutcliffe. Harmondsworth, England: Penguin, 1968.

Deutsch, H. (1942). Some forms of emotional disturbance and their relationship to schizophrenia. *Psychoanalytic Quarterly* 11:301–321.

Eibl-Eibesfeldt, I. (1970). *Ethology: The Biology of Behaviour.* New York: Holt.

Ekman, P. (1983). Autonomic nervous activity distinguishes among emotions. *Science* 221:1208–1210.

Ekman, P., and Friesen, W. (1975). *Unmasking the Face.* Englewood Cliffs, NJ: Prentice-Hall.

Ekman, P., Friesen, W., and Ellsworth, P. (1972). *Emotion in the Human Face: Guidelines for Research and Integration of Findings.* New York: Pergamon.

Eliot, T. S. (1932). Tradition and the individual talent. In *The Sacred Wood.* London: Methuen.

Ellenberger, H. F. (1970). *The Discovery of the Unconscious.* London: Allen Lane Press.

Elson, M., ed. (1987). *The Kohut Seminars on Self Psychology and Psychotherapy with Adolescents and Young Adults.* New York: Norton.

Emde, R. (1983). The prerepresentational self and its affective core. *Psychoanalytic Study of the Child* 38:165–192. New Haven CT: Yale University Press.

Erasmus, D. (1511). *In Praise of Folly.* Trans. H. H. Hudson. Princeton, NJ: Princeton University Press, 1970.

Flavell, J. (1968). *The Development of Role-Taking and Communications Skills in Children.* New York: Wiley.

Fantz, R. (1963). Pattern vision in new-born infants. *Science* 140:296–297.

_____ (1965). Visual perception from birth as shown by pattern selectivity. *Annals of New York Academy of Science* 118:793–814.

Freud, A. (1966). *The Ego and the Mechanisms of Defense.* Revised Edition. New York: International Universities Press.

Freud, S. (1905). Fragment of an analysis of a case of hysteria. *Standard Edition* 7:7–122. London: Hogarth, 1953.

_____ (1914). Remembering, repeating and working through. *Standard Edition* 12:145–156. London: Hogarth, 1958.

_____ (1920–1922). Two encyclopaedia articles. *Standard Edition* 18. Hogarth: London.

_____ (1925). An autobiographical study. *Standard Edition* 20.

_____ (1939). An outline of psychoanalysis. *Standard Edition* 23. London: Hogarth.

Friedman, J., Horvath, T., and Meares, R. (1974). Tobacco smoking and a stimulus-barrier. *Nature* 248:455–456.

Gallup, C. G. (1970). Chimpanzees: self recognition. *Science* 167:86–87.

Garvey, C. (1977). *Play.* Cambridge, MA: Harvard University Press.

Gill, M. (1985). The interactional aspect of transference. In *The Transference in Psychotherapy: Clinical Management,* ed. E. A. Schwaber. New York: International Universities Press.

Glasser, M. (1986). Identification and its vicissitudes as observed in the perversions. *International Journal of Psycho-Analysis* 67:9–17.

Goldberg, A. (1983). Self psychology and alternative perspectives on internalization. In *Reflections on Self Psychology,* ed. J. Lichtenberg and S. Kaplan. Hillsdale, NJ: Analytic Press.

_____ (1988). *A Fresh Look at Psychoanalysis: The View from Self Psychology.* Hillsdale, NJ: Analytic Press.

Goldstein, W. (1991). Clarification of projective identification. *American Journal of Psychiatry* 148:153–161.

Gopnik, A., and Astington, J. W. (1988). Children's understanding of representational change and its relation to the understanding of false belief and the appearance-reality distinction. *Child Development* 59:26–37.

Gosse, E. (1907). *Father and Son.* Harmondsworth, England: Penguin, 1983.

Gray, C. (1986). *The Russian Experiment in Art 1863–1922.* London: Thames & Hudson.

Gruber, H., and Vonèche, J. (1977). *The Essential Piaget.* New York: Basic Books.

Hadamard, J. (1945). *An Essay on the Psychology of Invention in the Mathematical Field.* Princeton, NJ: Princeton University Press.

Harter, S. (1983). Developmental perspectives on the self system. In *Handbook of Child Psychology,* vol. 4, ed. P. Mussen. New York: Wiley.

Hartmann, H. (1939). *Ego Psychology and the Problem of Adaption.* New York: International Universities Press, 1958.

Havens, L. (1978). Explorations in the uses of language in psychotherapy: simple empathic statements. *Psychiatry* 41:336–345.

_____ (1979). Explorations in the uses of language in psychotherapy: complex empathic statements. *Psychiatry* 42:40–48.

Herman, J., Perry, J., and van der Kolk, D. (1989). Childhood trauma in borderline personality disorder. *American Journal of Psychiatry* 146:490–495.

Hobson, R. F. (1985). *Forms of Feeling: The Heart of Psychotherapy.* London: Tavistock.

Hoffmann, M. (1978). Toward a theory of empathic arousal and development. In *The Development of Affect,* ed. M. Lewis and L. Rosenblum. New York: Plenum.

Horton, P., Louy, J., and Coppotillo, H. (1974). Personality disorder and transitional relatedness. *Archives of General Psychiatry* 30:618–622.

Horvath, T., Friedman, J., and Meares, R. (1980). Attention in hysteria: a study of Janet's hypothesis by means of habituation and arousal measures. *American Journal of Psychiatry* 137:217–220.

Horvath, T., and Meares, R. (1979). The sensory filter in schizophrenia: a study of habituation, arousal and the dopamine hypothesis. *British Journal of Psychiatry* 134:39–45.

Huizinga, J. (1938). *Homo Ludens: A Study of the Play Element in Culture.* London: Maurice Temple Smith, 1970.

Izard, C. (1971). *The Face of Emotion.* Meredith, NY: Appleton-Century-Crofts.

Jacobson, E. (1964). *The Self and the Object World.* New York: International Universities Press.

James, W. (1892). *Psychology: Briefer Course.* London: Macmillan.

Johnson, T. (1988). Child perpetrators—children who molest other children: preliminary findings. *Child Abuse and Neglect* 12:219–229.

Jung, C. G. (1935). The Tavistock lectures. In *The Symbolic Life: Collected Works*, vol. 18. London: Routledge & Kegan Paul.

―――― (1953). The persona as segment of the collective psyche. In *Two Essays of Analytical Psychology: Collected Works*, vol. 7, London: Routledge & Kegan Paul.

―――― (1954). The practice of psychotherapy. In *Collected Works*, vol. 16, London: Routledge & Kegan Paul.

―――― (1961). *Memories, Dreams and Reflections.* New York: Pantheon.

Kagan, J. (1981). *The Second Year: The Emergence of Self Awareness.* Cambridge, MA: Harvard University Press.

Kail, R. (1984). *The Development of Memory in Children.* New York: W. H. Freeman and Company.

Kernberg, O. (1968). The treatment of patients with borderline personality organization. *International Journal of Psycho-Analysis* 49:600–619.

―――― (1975). *Borderline Conditions and Pathological Narcissism.* New York: Jason Aronson.

―――― (1984). *Severe Personality Disorder.* New Haven: Yale University Press.

Klaus, M. (1975). Human behaviour following delivery: is this species specific? In *The Parent–Infant Interaction*, ed. M. Hofer and R. Porter. Amsterdam: Excerpta Medica.

Klee, P. (1964). *The Diaries of Paul Klee: 1898–1918*, ed. F. Klee. Berkeley, CA: University of California Press.

Klein, M. (1955). On identification. In *Envy and Gratitude and Other Works: 1946–1963*, pp. 141–175. London: Hogarth, 1975.

Kohler, W. (1925). *The Mentality of Apes.* London: Kegan Paul.

Kohut, H. (1959). Introspection, empathy and psychoanalysis. *Journal of the American Psychoanalytic Association* 7:459–482.

―――― (1971). *The Analysis of the Self.* New York: International Universities Press.

―――― (1977). *The Restoration of the Self.* New York: International Universities Press.

―――― (1984). *How Does Analysis Cure?* Ed. A. G. Goldberg. Chicago: University of Chicago Press.

Konishi, M. (1985). Birdsong: from behaviour to neuron. *Annual Review of Neuroscience* 8:125–170.

Kris, E. (1951). Ego psychology and interpretation in psychoanalytic therapy. *Psychoanalytic Quarterly* 20:21–25.

_____ (1983). *Free Association.* New Haven, CT: Yale University Press.

Lacan, J. (1977). *Ecrits: A Selection.* Trans. A. Sheridan. London: Tavistock.

Levenson, E. (1972). *The Fallacy of Understanding.* New York: Basic Books.

Levi-Strauss, C. (1979). *Myth and Meaning.* New York: Schocken.

Lewis, M. (1969). A developmental study of information processing within the first three years of life: response decrement to a redundant signal. *Monographs of the Society for Research in Child Development* 34, No. 9 (whole No. 133).

_____ (1990). Self knowledge and social development in early life. In *Handbook of Social Psychology,* ed. L. Pervin. New York: Guilford.

_____ (1992). *Shame: The Exposed Self.* New York: The Free Press.

Lewis, M., and Brooks-Gunn, J. (1979). Social cognition and the acquisition of self. New York: Plenum.

Lewis, M., and Gunn, J. (1978). Self-knowledge and emotional development. In: *The Development of Affect,* ed. M. Lewis and L. Rosenblum. New York: Plenum.

Lichtenberg, J. (1983). *Psychoanalysis and Infant Research.* Hillsdale, NJ: Analytic Press.

_____ (1989). *Psychoanalysis and Motivation.* Hillsdale, NJ: Analytic Press.

Lichtenberg, J., Bornstein, M., and Silver, D., eds. (1984). *Empathy,* vol. 1. Hillsdale, NJ: Analytic Press.

Lifton, R. J. (1976). *The Life of the Self.* New York: Simon and Schuster.

Locke, J. L., and Pearson, D. (1990). The linguistic significance of babbling: evidence from a tracheotomized infant. *Journal of Child Language* 17:1–16.

Ludolph, P., Westen, D., Misle, B., Jackson, A., et al. (1990). The borderline diagnosis in adolescents: symptoms and developmental history. *American Journal of Psychiatry* 147:470–476.

MacFarlane, J. (1975). Olfaction in the development of social preferences in the human neonate. In *Parent–Infant Interaction,* ed. M. Hofer. Amsterdam: Elsevier.

Mahler, M., Pine, F., and Bergmann, A. (1975). *The Psychological Birth of the Human Infant.* London: Hutchinson.

Mandler, J. M. (1984). Representation and recall in infancy. In *Infant Memory,* ed. M. Moscovitch. New York: Plenum.

Matas, L., Arend, R., and Sroufe, L. A. (1978). Continuity of adaptation in the second year: the relationship between quality of attachment and later competence. *Child Development* 49:547–556.

McFarlane, A. (1974). If a smile is so important. . . . *New Scientist* 62:174.

McLean, P. (1969). The paranoid streak in man. In *Beyond Reductionism*, ed. A. Koestler and J. Smythies. London: Hutchinson. (Radius edition cited here, 1972).

—— (1986). Culminating developments in the evolution of the limbic system: the thalamocingulate division. In *The Limbic System: Functional Organization and Clinical Disorders*, ed. B. Doane and K. Livington. New York: Raven.

Meares, A. (1961). What makes the patient better? *Lancet* 1:1280–1281.

—— (1962). What makes the patient better? *Lancet* 1:151–153.

Meares, R. (1973a). Beckett, Sarraute, and the perceptual experience of schizophrenia. *Psychiatry* 36:61–69.

—— (1973b). Two kinds of groups. *British Journal of Medical Psychology* 46:373–379.

—— (1976). The secret. *Psychiatry* 39:258–265.

—— (1977). *The Pursuit of Intimacy: An Approach to Psychotherapy.* Melbourne: Nelson.

—— (1980). Body feelings in human relations: the possible examples of Brancusi and Giacometti. *Psychiatry* 43:160–167.

—— (1981). On saying good-bye before death. *Journal of the American Medical Association* 246:1227–1229.

—— (1983). Keats and the "impersonal" therapist: a note on empathy and the therapeutic screen. *Psychiatry* 46:73–82.

—— (1985). Metaphor and reality. *Contemporary Psychoanalysis* 21:425–445.

—— (1986). On the ownership of thought: an approach to the origins of separation anxiety. *Psychiatry* 21:545–559.

—— (1987). The secret and the self: on a new direction in psychotherapy. *Australian and New Zealand Journal of Psychiatry* 21:545–559.

—— (1988). The secret, lies and the paranoid process. *Contemporary Psychoanalysis* 24:650–666.

—— (1990). The fragile spielraum: an approach to transmuting internalization. In *The Realities of Transference: Progress in Self Psychology*, vol. 6, ed. A. Goldberg, pp. 69–89. Hillsdale, NJ: Analytic Press.

—— (1992). Transference and the playspace. *Contemporary Psychoanalysis* 28:32–49.

Meares, R., and Grose, D. (1978). On depersonalization in adolescence: a consideration from the viewpoint of habituation and "identity". *British Journal of Medical Psychology* 51:335–342.

Meares, R., and Hobson, R. (1977). The persecutory therapist. *British Journal of Medical Psychology* 50:349–359.

Meares, R., and Horvath, T. (1972). "Acute" and "chronic" hysteria. *British Journal of Psychiatry* 121:653–657.

Meares, R., and Orlay, W. (1988). On self boundary: a study of the development of the concept of secrecy. *British Journal of Medical Psychology* 1:305–316.

Meares, R., Penman, R., Milgrom-Friedman, J., and Baker, K. (1982). Some origins of the 'difficult' child. The Brazelton scale and the mother's view of her new born's character. *British Journal of Medical Psychology* 55:77–86.

Meltzoff, A. N. (1988). Infant imitation after a one-week delay: long-term memory for novel acts and multiple stimuli. *Developmental Psychology* 24:470–476.

Melzack, R., and Chapman, C. (1973). Psychologic aspects of pain. *Postgraduate Medicine* 53:69–75.

Melzack, R., and Wall, P. (1982). *The Challenge of Pain*. New York: Penguin.

Merskey, H. (1980). The nature of pain. In *Pain: Meaning and Management*, ed. W. Smith, A. Merskey, and S. Gross. New York: Spectrum.

Miller, H. (1965). *Tropic of Cancer*. London: Panther.

Miltner, W., Johnson, R., Jr., Braun, C., and Larbig, W. (1989). Somatosensory event-related potentials to painful and non-painful stimuli: effects of attention. *Pain* 38:303–312.

Mishima, Y. (1958). *Confessions of a Mask*. Trans. M. Weatherby. New York: New Directions.

Modell, A. (1963). Primitive object relationships and the predisposition to schizophrenia. *International Journal of Psychoanalysis* 44:282–291.

_____ (1976). "The holding environment" and the therapeutic action of psychoanalysis. *Journal of the American Psychoanalytic Association* 24:285–308.

Money, J., and Ehrhardt, A. (1972). *Man and Woman: Boy and Girl*. Baltimore: Johns Hopkins University Press.

Morris, H., Gunderson, J., and Zanarini, M. (1986). Transitional object use and borderline pathology. *American Journal of Psychiatry* 143:1534–1538.

Murphy, L. (1972). Infants' play and cognitive development. In *Play and Development*, ed. M. Piers. New York: Norton.

Murray, L., and Trevarthen, C. (1985). Emotional regulation of interactions between two-month-olds and their mothers. In *Social Perception in Infants*, ed. T. Field and N. Fox. Norwood, NJ: Ablex.

Nelson, K. (1984). The transition from infant to child memory. In *Infant Memory*, ed. M. Moscovitch. New York: Plenum.

Nelson, K., and Ross, G. (1980). The generalities and specifics of long-term memory in infants and young children. In *Children's Memory: New Directions for Child Development*, no. 10, ed. M. Perlmutter. San Francisco: Jossey-Bass.

Nicolson, N., ed. (1975). *The Flight of the Mind: The Letters of Virginia Woolf.* Vol. 1: *1888–1912.* London: Hogarth.

Nin A. (1931–1934). *The Diary of Anais Nin.* Vol. 1. Ed. G. Stuhlmann. New York: Harcourt, Brace & World, 1966.

—— (1939–1944). *The Diary of Anais Nin.* Vol. 3. Ed. G. Stuhlmann. New York: Harcourt, Brace, Jovanovich, 1969.

—— (1969). *The Diary of Anais Nin.* Vol. 3. ed. G. Stuhlmann. New York: Harcourt, Brace, Jovanovich.

Ogden, T. (1982). *Projective Identification and Psychotherapeutic Technique.* New York: Jason Aronson.

Olds, J., and Milner, P. (1954). Positive reinforcement produced by electrical stimulation of the septal area and other regions of rat brain. *Journal of Comparative Physiology and Psychology* 47:419–427.

Olinick, S. (1984). A critique of empathy and sympathy. In *Empathy*, vol. 1, ed. J. Lichtenberg, M. Bornstein, and D. Silver. Hillsdale, NJ: Analytic Press.

Olson, G. M., and Strauss, M. S. (1984). The development of infant memory. In *Infant Memory*, ed. M. Moscovitch. New York: Plenum.

Ornstein, P. (1985). The thwarted need to grow: clinical-theoretical issues in the self-object transference. In *The Transference in Psychotherapy: Clinical Management*, ed. E. A. Schwaber. New York: International Universities Press.

Patterson, A. B. (Banjo) (1895). "The Man from Snowy River." In *The Collected Verse of A. B. Patterson.* Melbourne, Australia: Angus and Robertson.

Penman, R., Meares, R., Baker, K., and Milgrom-Friedman, J. (1983). Synchrony in mother–infant interaction: a possible neurophysiological base. *British Journal of Medical Psychology* 56:1–7.

Penman, R., Meares, R., and Milgrom-Friedman, J. (1981). The mother's role in the development of object competency. *Archives de Psychologie* 49:247–265.

Perner, J., Leekam, S. R., and Wimmer, H. (1987). Three-year-olds' difficulty with false belief: the case for conceptual deficit. *British Journal of Developmental Psychology* 5:125–137.

Piaget, J. (1929). *The Child's Conception of the World.* London: Routledge & Kegan Paul.

_____ (1932). *The Moral Judgement of the Child*. London: Routledge & Kegan Paul.

_____ (1951). *Play, Dreams and Imitation in Childhood*. London: Heinemann.

_____ (1954). *The Construction of Reality in the Child*. New York: Basic Books.

_____ (1959). *The Language and Thought of the Child*. London: Routledge & Kegan Paul.

Pine, F. (1986). On the development of the "borderline-child-to-be." *American Journal of Orthopsychiatry* 56:450–457.

Plaut, A. (1966). Reflections about not being able to imagine. *Journal of Analytical Psychology* 11:113–133.

Rhys, J. (1967). *Good Morning Midnight*. London: Deutsch.

Robson, P. (1988). Self-esteem—a psychiatric view. *British Journal of Psychiatry* 153:6–15.

Russell, B. (1971). *Autobiography of Bertrand Russell*. Vol. 1. London: Allen and Unwin.

St. Barbe Baker, R. (1970). *My Life, My Trees*. Scotland: Findhorn.

Sandler, J., and Rosenblatt, B. (1962). The concept of the representational world. *Psychoanalytic Study of the Child* 17:128–148. New York: International Universities Press.

Schaffer, H. (1971). *The Growth of Sociability*. Hammondsworth, England: Penguin.

Scherer, K., and Oshinsky, J. (1977). Cue utilization in emotion attribution from auditory stimuli. *Motivation and Emotion* 1:331–346.

Schwaber, E. (1983). A particular perspective on analytic listening. *Psychoanalytic Study of the Child* 38:519–546. New Haven, CT: Yale University Press.

Schwartz, A., Campos, J., and Baisel, E. (1973). The visual cliff: cardiac and behavioural correlates of the deep and shallow sides at 5 and 9 months of age. *Journal of Experimental Child Psychology* 15:86–99.

Screech, M. (1988). *Erasmus: Ecstasy and the Praise of Folly*. London: Penguin.

Simmel, G. (1964). *The Sociology of George Simmel*. Ed. K. H. Wolff. Glencoe, IL: The Free Press.

Sokolov, Y. N. (1960). Neuronal models and the orienting reflex. In *The Central Nervous System and Behaviour*, ed. M. Brazier. New York: J. Macey Foundation.

Sorce, J., and Emde, R. (1981). Mother's presence is not enough. *Developmental Psychology* 17:737–745.

Sorce, J., Emde, R., Campos, J., and Klinnet, M. (1985). Maternal emotional signalling: its effect on the visual cliff behaviour of 1-year-olds. *Developmental Psychology* 21:195–200.

Spitz, R. (1965). *The First Year of Life.* New York: International Universities Press.

Steele, B. (1986). Notes on the lasting effects of early child abuse throughout the life cycle. *Child Abuse and Neglect* 10:283–291.

Stekel, W. (1924). The polyphony of thought. In *The Organization and Pathology of Thought: Selected Sources.* Trans. and ed. D. Rapaport. New York: Columbia University Press, 1951.

Stern, D. (1985). *The Interpersonal World of the Infant.* New York: Basic Books.

Stevenson, J., and Meares, R. (1992). An outcome study of psychotherapy in borderline personality disorder. *American Journal of Psychiatry* 149:358–362.

Stolorow, R. (1986). Critical reflections on the theory of self psychology: an inside view. *Psychoanalytic Inquiry* 6:387–402.

Stolorow, R., and Atwood, G. (1992). *Contexts of Being: The Intersubjective Foundations of Psychological Life.* Hillsdale, NJ: Analytic Press.

Stolorow, R., Brandchaft, B., and Atwood, G. (1987). *Psychoanalytic Treatment: an Intersubjective Approach.* Hillsdale, NJ: Analytic Press.

Strachey, J. (1961). Editorial note. *Standard Edition* 19:8.

Sullivan, H. S. (1953). *The Interpersonal Theory of Psychiatry.* New York: Norton.

Tichener, E. (1905). *Experimental Psychology: A Manual of Laboratory Experiments.* New York: MacMillan.

Trevarthen, C. (1974). Conversations with a two-month-old. *New Scientist* 62:230–235.

———— (1983). Emotions in infancy: regulators of contacts and relationships with persons. In *Approaches to Emotion,* ed. K. Scherer and P. Ekman. Hillsdale, NJ: Lawrence Erlbaum.

———— (1987). Mind in infancy. In *The Oxford Companion to the Mind,* ed. R. L. Gregory. Oxford, England: Oxford University Press.

Vygotsky, L. S. (1962). *Thought and Language.* Ed. and Trans. E. Hanfmann and G. Vakar. Cambridge, MA: M.I.T. Press.

Winnicott, D. W. (1948). Reparation in respect of mother's organized defence against depression. In *Collected Papers: Through Paediatrics to Psychoanalysis.* London: Tavistock, 1958.

———— (1949). Mind and its relation to the Psyche-Soma. In *Collected Papers: Through Paediatrics to Psychoanalysis.* London: Tavistock, 1958.

———— (1950–1955). Aggression in relation to emotional development. In *Collected Papers: Through Paediatrics to Psychoanalysis.* London: Tavistock, 1958.

_____ (1952). Psychoses and child care. In *Collected Papers: Through Paediatrics to Psychoanalysis*. London: Tavistock, 1958.

_____ (1953). Transitional objects and transitional phenomena. In *Playing and Reality*. Hammondsworth, England: Penguin, 1974.

_____ (1956). Primary maternal preoccupation. In *Collected Papers: Through Paediatrics to Psychoanalysis*. London: Tavistock, 1958.

_____ (1958). The capacity to be alone. In *The Maturational Processes and the Facilitating Environment*. New York: International Universities Press.

_____ (1960). Ego distinction in terms of true and false self. In *The Maturational Processes and the Facilitating Environment*. New York: International Universities Press, 1965.

_____ (1962). Ego integration in child development. In *The Maturational Processes and the Facilitating Environment*. New York: International Universities Press, 1965.

_____ (1963). Communicating and not communicating leading to a study of certain opposites. In *The Maturational Processes and the Facilitating Environment*. New York: International Universities Press, 1965.

_____ (1974). *Playing and Reality*. Hammondsworth, England: Penguin.

Wolf, E. (1988). *Treating the Self: Elements of Clinical Self Psychology*. New York: Guilford.

Woolf, V. (1925). *The Common Reader*. London: Hogarth.

Wundt, W. (1904). *Principles of Physiological Psychology*. New York: MacMillan.

Wylie, R. (1979). *The Self Concept*. Vol. 2. *Theory and Research on Selected Topics*. Lincoln, NE: University of Nebraska Press.

Young, J. Z. (1974). *Introduction to the Study of Man*. Oxford, England: Oxford University Press.

Zanarini, M., Gunderson, J., Marino, M., et al. (1989). Childhood experiences of borderline patients. *Comprehensive Psychiatry* 30:18–25.

Zigmond, R., Nottebohm, F., and Pfaff, D. (1973). Androgen concentrating cells in the mid-brain of the song-bird. *Science* 179:1005–1007.

INDEX